love and hate

in the

HEARTLAND

Also by Mark Phillips:

My Father's Cabin

love and hate
in the
HEARTLAND

dispatches from forgotten america

MARK PHILLIPS

Skyhorse Publishing

Skyhorse Publishing books may be purchased in bulk at special discounts for sales promotion, corporate gifts, fund-raising, or educational purposes. Special editions can also be created to specifications. For details, contact the Special Sales Department, Skyhorse Publishing, 307 West 36th Street, 11th Floor, New York, NY 10018 or info@skyhorsepublishing.com.

Skyhorse® and Skyhorse Publishing® are registered trademarks of Skyhorse Publishing, Inc.®, a Delaware corporation.

Visit our website at www.skyhorsepublishing.com.

10 9 8 7 6 5 4 3 2 1

Library of Congress Cataloging-in-Publication Data is available on file.

Cover design by Rain Saukas
Cover photo credit: iStockphoto.com

ISBN: 978-1-51073-498-2
Ebook ISBN: 978-1-51073-500-2

Printed in the United States of America

In memory of Kim

ACKNOWLEDGMENTS

I am grateful to the helpful and patient editors at journals where portions of this book were previously published. Many of these essays originally appeared in different form in *Commonweal, Salon, Blueline, The Sun, Notre Dame Magazine, North Dakota Quarterly, The Phoenix, J Journal: New Writing on Justice,* and my memoir, *My Father's Cabin.* Also, I am grateful to the authors whose books I consulted while writing three of my essays here: Laurence Marc Hauptman (*In the Shadow of Kinzua*), Joy Bilharz (*The Allegheny Senecas and Kinzua Dam*), Peter J. Thuesen (*Predestination*), Paul K. Jewett (*Election and Predestination*), Jeffrey Burton Russell (*Mephistopheles* and *The Devil*), and Maximilian Rudwin (*The Devil in Legend and Literature*). Finally, and for numerous reasons, I thank the Phillips clan, Doug Whiteman, Joe Craig, Tony Lyons, Lilly Golden, Kerry Temple, and Bridget Kehrer. And especially Athena.

And a note on spelling:

The place-name *Allegheny* sometimes appears in this book as *Allegany.* I live on the Allegheny Plateau and near the Allegheny

River and Reservoir, but also near the town, county, state park, and Native American territory given the name *Allegany*, a regional variation of *Allegheny*.

CONTENTS

PREFACE

"Don't let them make you forget where you came from," my father said to me when I was earning a teaching degree. He also said, "Study hard. You won't make a living by writing except in your dreams." I didn't think he needed to worry: I was proud of where I came from. And I had no intention of ever going back.

Two decades later, during one of my periods of unemployment, I joined my writer friend, Tom—who had not yet begun to make a living by writing—at a bar where free Buffalo-style chicken wings baited customers into buying expensive beer. At a table beneath the noise and flashing of a television, his and my literary insights—watered by the two glasses of beer that each of us purchased—grew until a waiter encouraged us to depart the premises because we had been inhaling so many free wings that he feared we would bankrupt the boss. We soon resumed our conversation back at Tom's kitchen table, also known as the salon, where the beer was cheaper. When we eventually got on the subject of what hard work writing is, Tom's wife, Fran, couldn't bear to hear another word of nonsense from a pair of unemployed typists. "You guys sound stupid," she said. "The farmers around here, they work hard. They're working before it's light out and work until after dark. They all get bad backs and bad hips and they keep going. What are you guys going to get? Hemorrhoids?"

Maybe I *was* forgetting where I came from.

Where I came from was the town of Pendleton, New York, twenty miles from Buffalo, and where the Oklahoma City bomber, Timothy McVeigh, grew up. McVeigh's father worked on the mass-production line at a radiator plant operated by General Motors, and my father welded at a coal-fired power plant just outside of Buffalo. General Motors has since sold the radiator plant, and the power plant is now idle.

Everyone knows about the manufacturing and employment changes in America; the *Wall Street Journal* has faithfully reported the effects on stocks and bonds. Damage to workers and their families has been covered all along by certain rust-belt newspapers, such as the *Buffalo News* and *Detroit Free Press*, but for the most part the suffering of the downsized and dispossessed was ignored until the ascendancy of Donald Trump to the presidency, when the victims became categorized as "the Trump voter." They were also dubbed "the rural white voter," although most working-class people live in cities and suburbs; and in rural America, such as the northern Alleghenies, where I've lived for thirty-seven years now—in the little town of Ischua, seventy miles south of Pendleton—a Trump supporter in a house trailer might live on the same road as a liberal in a $200,000 renovated Victorian. Rural whites, whether they are rich or poor, or have a college degree, medical insurance, or a religion, all are lumped together as "the Trump voter." This tells me that when someone different is elected president, and Trump's kind of lip-servicing of rural Americans can no longer be mistaken as genuine, most of the nation will feel free to forget about us in the hinterlands—whoever any of us really are.

Since that night at Tom's kitchen table, I've tried to remember where I came from, and yet I couldn't go back to the old working-class life even if I wished. To borrow an expression from Gertrude Stein, these days "there is no there there."

What's more, the "there there" was never as I used to believe. Even when America's factories were at full production and the union was king, working-class whites on the whole were never exactly the kind of people that most of us like to think they are. Although stubbornly proud, for a long while now the working class, whether in the city or suburb or countryside, has been neglected by our government and mocked by my fellow college-educated liberals—and yet, despite their frequent generosity to each other and their belief that they are fair-minded folk, many of the white working class mock, resent, hate, or prefer to neglect their fellow struggling Americans whose skin is darker.

Dad would be proud of what I've become, but with ambivalence. I'm a full-time teacher and tutor in the Higher Education Opportunity Program at a small Franciscan college, and am blessed to know my students—a belief of mine that would have troubled my dad. Each of them is a recipient of a scholarship for those who without financial help would be unable to attend college, and since most of my students have brown skin, my father would have regarded them as confirmation of his belief that whites are discriminated against. The students are one of the reasons I have a job, and have taught me more than I them. Some years ago, a student and I were discussing the snarling and murderous racism evoked by portions of Richard Wright's *Black Boy*, and I said,

"The strange thing about the bigots in my own family is that otherwise they're decent people."

"A decent bigot," she said. "Isn't that an oxymoron?"

I answered with one word, and became silent on the subject of decency and bigots, until now.

This book travels the American heartland, by which I mean an experiential and emotional rather than geographic place. The personal and narrative essays that comprise this book are linked by my now deceased grandparents, parents, aunts, and uncles; my living wife and two children; my friends and neighbors; and my former and current selves. Whether flesh or ghosts walking the land I call home, they tell me stories of love and hate.

And of Donald Trump—and of life, I hope, forever beyond his reach.

WAITING FOR TRUMP

WHEN WE HAD IT MADE IN AMERICA

When I believed my country was the land of opportunity, its clattering factories and smoky mills used electricity generated at the power plant where my father worked as a welder. He wore a hard hat and belonged to the union, and I believed he was as mighty as our young president who had stared down Khrushchev. He was still at work when my sisters and I climbed off the school bus in the afternoons, but our mother was there to greet us in her sparkling disinfected kitchen, and I believed she was as fulfilled as a saint. In that time and that place, our family was protected by steel parentheses, made in America, from a hurtling, changing story that we couldn't know.

Yet even back then—when the shelves in the stores weren't yet packed with Chinese products, the factories weren't moving to Mexico and Malaysia, and "downsizing" wasn't a word—my grandfather, Barley Phillips, no longer believed in forever, not exactly, not for him; though for the nation, yes, for whatever immortality can be obtained through hard work, yes. Like his brothers and father, Barley had been an iron worker, though eventually he took a safer job as a maintenance foreman in a power plant he'd helped build. My father worked in the same power plant, and someday, if I had what it took, I too could make a living in the coal and fly ash in the bowels of the plant or by clinging with skill to the swaying skeleton of a rising bridge or skyscraper. Of course I would have what it took. Of course one of my kinsmen would speak to a boss on my behalf. *Let there be work.* Of course.

By the time I turned seven years old my grandfather had retired from his job as a foreman at the plant, sold his house in Buffalo, and was living with Grandma in the countryside. Along with a small house, his property included a chicken coop, workshop, empty barn, and eleven acres of abandoned cropland. Because I spent so many evenings and weekends with him while Dad worked overtime at the plant, I felt closer to Grandpa than to my often-absent father. Once when Barley was preparing to smoke wasps out of his workshop, he pointed above the workbench to a large framed photograph of a man with thick frosty hair and bushy eyebrows, a long nose, a handlebar mustache, and a no-nonsense expression. He told me the man was his father, who had been "a hardworking blacksmith and then an iron worker." Although Grandpa didn't keep the photograph in his house, he hadn't discarded it; he kept it in his workshop as if his memories of his father were inextricably tied to labor.

In the yard on warm summer evenings, sitting in metal lawn chairs or stretched out on the grass in the shade of pear trees, near the hand-operated water pump and the metal pink flamingos and the free-range chickens stalking clover and bugs, Grandpa sipped beer and I gulped pop and we talked until dark. He gently teased me, encouraged me to talk about my life, and listened sincerely. But because I was too young to believe it, he never told me what he had learned about the mortality of men and women, telling me instead about the heirloom of work. We drifted over sunken family legends, but when stories were told the legends rose. Maybe you know them. If your family was among the lucky, you can substitute your own surnames and ethnic backgrounds, change some other details, and you know them: the Welsh horse-trading great-great-grandfather who settled in Ireland. The Welsh-Irish great-grandfather who ran away from the farm to work in the Belfast shipyards and then, when work slowed, sailed to North America and became a blacksmith in booming Buffalo. The grandfather who became an ironworker in Buffalo even though his father and two of his older brothers had fallen to their deaths on the job—but who, after helping to build a power plant, took a job there. The father who became a welder at the same plant. All of them always chasing work, capturing it, becoming better. In these legends, equal opportunity laws don't exist, the wife stays home, the kids do their homework, each generation buys a bigger house than the one before, and the economy grows stronger forever.

One evening while my father was driving us home from the plant—where I was working during my summer break from college—he glanced over at me and said, apologetically, "When you knew your grandfather, he was old. He wasn't the man he used to be." By then the factories in Buffalo were beginning to close, and Dad had been diagnosed with terminal cancer.

At eighteen years old, my father was assigned to the Utility Department. Whatever messes occurred around the plant were cleaned up by the Utility laborers. The other workers called them "the Shit Crew." In the Coal Department, to which most Utility laborers hoped to be promoted, the work was just as dirty but the pay better—so the utility men waited and hoped for someone in Coal to retire or die.

On his second morning on the Shit Crew my father climbed up an iron ladder to a cramped four-foot-high area above a boiler. Most of the sweltering space was deep in leaked fly ash. Crouched on his hands and knees, he surveyed the space: a long vacuum hose connected to the stack system of the plant lay in fresh ash that had accumulated since Monday, when he left much of the area clean. He put on goggles, then a respirator. Immediately, his perspiring face felt uncomfortable within the rubber, and he began the labored deep breathing necessary to obtain a sufficient air supply. Pushing off his hard hat, he crawled further in and picked up the eight-inch circumference hose. He handled the hose gently, but the light ash began to fill the air and adhere to his sweaty work-suit and skin. A few minutes later another Utility worker, with a shovel, joined him, and the air quickly became saturated as the two men, shoveling and vacuuming, worked blindly in a gray cloud of decently paying hell.

After several months in Utility, he was trained to weld and was promoted directly to the Maintenance Department, where his father was a foreman. My father worked in the same noise and heat and dirt and crawl spaces as in Utility, and his ankles and wrists were burned by molten metal splattering into his shoes and gloves, but he was now a skilled laborer and problem solver, with job security and a fair paycheck. Now he was "set for life." And he married Eva Wagner, who was a telephone operator, although they would need to live with his parents for a year before they could afford a house of their own. When he perspired at the wedding reception, fly ash and coal dust, embedded deep in his pores, gradually graced his white shirt gray.

The plant was a concrete and steel and red-brick building that rose several stories in a jumble of variously shaped and sized tiers. My father's job was so much a part of our family conversation and so shaped our lives that the words "the plant" always registered like the name of a boss, as if my mother and father were talking about someone powerful who was named Mr. Plant. Once my father rented a small motorboat and took me fishing on the Niagara River. He anchored the boat near the water-intake building of the plant, and I saw that the closer a brick tier was to the river, the squatter it was, as if Mr. Plant were crouched forward to drink. The river swirled where water was guzzled in and out of the plant to cool machinery and to become the steam that spun the turbines and passed out through submerged pipes. The humming of the jumble of outside transformers rose and fell, like troubled breathing. Long trucks were lined up in the coal yard, dumping black food near the mechanical feeders; other long trucks were carrying away what my father told me was fly ash, the waste matter. Mr. Plant belched steamy heat and ireful smoke into the sky. I tried to see what was in the belly of the big boss, but the windows were too grimy, the eyes too glazed.

My father always took one of his two weeks of vacation to hunt deer in November, and since he worked too much overtime at the plant to accomplish substantial household repairs and improvements at other times, he used his other week of vacation to labor at home in July or August. In 1958, so that my sister Kim and I need no longer share a bedroom, he used a week of vacation to convert our small living room into a bedroom and to begin building addition for a new and bigger living room. In 1959, he finished the living room and poured sidewalks. In 1960, he put on a new roof and remodeled the bathroom. Separately we were so busy—he with work and I with the childhood I felt was eternal—that at times we seemed, despite our love, to be mere acquaintances.

One evening a man entered our home without knocking. His clothing and skin were black. He laughed at my fright and failure to recognize him. The showers at the plant had been shut down for repairs.

What was it all for, the toiling, sacrificing, and saving in an imaginary paradise that would be lost? On a sticky summer evening my father and I, in the middle of the front lawn beneath a maple tree with lusterless leaves hanging still, sat in lawn chairs and rocked slightly on curved, springy legs. Nestlings chirped and robins hopped across the lawn. Throughout the neighborhood, men and children, and women after the kitchen work was done, all full with food, came outside. Children in bathing suits ran shouting through the arching spray of law sprinklers, fell, jumped up laughing with blades of grass sticking to their skin; others, including my sisters, migrated barefooted up the shoulder of the road, stepping gingerly on the gravel, carrying towels to visit friends who had small swimming pools. As the shadows stretched and the angling light became syrupy, the shouts and laughter reverberating off the encircled water of the above-ground pools faded into the chatter of children hiking home with bathing suits dripping and wet hair tangled. Adults carried lawn chairs into the garage, coiled their garden hoses, walked laggardly into sweltering houses. One by one the living room windows filled with yellow light. The heavy sky rumbled in the distance, the leaves rustled, and the air began to fill with the earthy odor of an approaching storm. Dad and I, who all evening had exchanged no more than a dozen words, stood up to go inside where Mom and my sisters had settled in front of the television.

Work granted a brief time and small place where the toiling, sacrificing, and saving could be forgotten.

My wife, Margaret, is a retired schoolteacher who earned a good living and now has a good pension. For a long time now I've been a writer, an occupation at which I earn satisfaction, and meanwhile have moved from low-paying job to low-paying job as factory grunt, childcare worker, swimming-pool installer, security guard, small-firm paralegal, and tutor of college students. One year when the Reunion Committee asked my high school classmates and me to report on our lives, to contribute something envious and upbeat to the reunion booklet, I wrote, "Mark Phillips lives off his wife."

Two decades ago when my daughter, Hope, was six years old, she began requesting a new type of bedtime story on evenings when I was not busy writing or working an evening shift. She would study the several framed photographs hanging on the living room wall before pointing to one and asking, "Tonight will you please tell me a story about that picture?" And after she was tucked in I would tell her a legend inspired by the photograph of her great-great-great-grandfather gripping the handles of a horse-drawn plow in the North of Ireland, or her grandfather wearing coal-blackened coveralls, or her mother holding her in front of our home when she was a newborn.

And once, after I finished telling her the legend of the sacrifices her mother and I made before we could afford to build our small home, my daughter asked, "Do you think I'll live here when I grow up?"

"Maybe."

"Forever?"

DON'T THEY TEACH THIS IN COLLEGE?

During one of his fifteen days of vacation from the dark heat of the power plant, on his way to the acres he had purchased in the hill country south of our home, land from which a spring flowed and kept full a pond cold enough for trout in all seasons, he gave advice to his son who was in danger of failing to graduate from high school. Between his moments of coughing up phlegm black with coal dust and cigarette tar, and swiping his mouth against his shirt sleeve, he said, as he had a number of times before, that I should go to college and become a teacher in order to have my summers off. He added, though, that to carry out such a plan I would need to cease taking so much time off from my high school studies.

My father was in his early forties and had worked overtime for decades. Yet in the jostling pickup he told me on our way to his forty acres that except for the truly poor he'd never known a dying person who wished to have made more money, and that instead the dying wished for more time with family or whatever else they truly loved. Although he knew he had cancer, and that it was inoperable and untreatable, he was driving to his land in order to labor there on a vacation day. To buy the land, he had needed to work long and hard, and now, to finish building his dream cabin in the country, he needed to work more. And to hurry. He expected me to work alongside.

At least, I saw it as work. I believe that in his way my father— who most likely had never read a poem or novel in his life— thought of himself when working with his hands as a poet of the School of Hard Knocks, his cabin a creation that would grace his lost time and the cancerous pain in his bones. I realize that more than a few MFA poets and professors of literature will sneer at my favorable comparison of an ordinary building, a small structure subject to decay, to a profound and beautiful poem; and yet, two decades after my father's death, I one morning found myself thinking about his creation. I was conversing with a guy who had retired early from his job as a phone company linesman, and I had hired to add on a bedroom to my home. His teenage son was with him when he said—I suspect more to the boy than me—"If I point up at a phone line and tell somebody I spliced that line, what does it mean to them? But if I point to an addition on a house where a family lives, and I say I built that, well, it means something."

I felt that the carpenter was no longer standing outside my home as he spoke, but inside. Come on in, he seemed to be saying to his son. It was what a good teacher of poetry might say to her class.

I took my father's advice. I liked the idea of time off during which I could stay out late on the town, sleep in, and compose doggerel. I passed chemistry and trigonometry the second time through, and was accepted by a college with low academic standards. I became a fairly good high school teacher, but I thought of teaching as work and longed all autumn, winter, and spring for my summers off. And yet these days I no longer think of teaching as work that I long to escape. I now teach at a college where many of my students are children of immigrants, and one afternoon a Dominican-American student told me that the reason he wanted a college degree and well-paying job was so that his parents could quit their minimum-wage jobs; and finally, I understood that teaching is not work. Not *that* kind of work, anyhow. It was work I could live in.

If a family in my neighborhood went to a restaurant, it usually signaled that a special occasion was at hand, such as the high school graduation of a child who would be attending college rather than following Dad into a plant or mill or Mom into the kitchen and laundry room. Most families didn't "do without," but they also didn't have much more than they needed. Except when my father owned the rusty pickup truck used to carry supplies to his cabin-in-progress—a truck he would later sell to a guy who fled town before the check bounced—I can't recall any family that owned two vehicles. Siblings of the same sex were expected to share a bedroom, as one of my friends and his three brothers did, their dirty clothing piled on the narrow floor space between the bunk beds abutting opposite walls, the mound of muddy and grassy denim and cotton providing a good cushion when each morning the brothers in the top bunks would ignore the ladder and leap down. Of course, women did the laundry. Women prepared the meals. Women changed the diapers. Women cleaned the house. Even the women who worked full time at Harrison Radiator, one of the few local industries that would hire them for jobs other than typing and cleaning, did most of the housework and childcare and cooking.

If women's liberation came late to my neighborhood, perhaps in small part it was because it was difficult to be envious of a man who came home coughing up foundry fumes or whose skin was yellowed by the chemical plant, and who, during weekends and vacations, had built the house the family lived in.

My uncle Al punched the time clock at the power plant for his first time a mere two mornings after his high school graduation, when my father was still a junior-high-school student. By the time America entered World War Two, Al had been trained to weld at the plant and therefore was eligible for a military deferment as a skilled employee of an essential industry; but he enlisted in the army anyhow, and was wounded in Germany. Before his wound healed, the war ended. Eventually he went back to work at the plant, welding broken-down machinery and leaky boilers until the day when his foreman—who had been deferred from military service—began to chew him out for loafing on the job. About the foreman's harangue, Al didn't tell me what he said in response. He told me only, "I didn't let him finish."

He walked midday from the massive oven that was the power plant, from its air peppered with fly ash and coal dust, from its rattling banging, whining conveyors and crushers and turbines, from its dingy lighting. The next morning, he went to work on a construction job as a steamfitter. When I was paying for my education by working summers at the plant, I was tempted to quit college to take a full-time job there—to endure where my paternal grandfather had until his retirement and my dying father had until he could no longer climb the stairs to the time clock each morning—though I might just as well have moved into a casket to lay in the dark and count the shovelfuls of dirt as they thumped and rattled the lid. "Come on, now," Al said. "Can you imagine walking into that place for the rest of your life? You better think, boy."

Back then it was an economic given that a lad could go to work where his grandfather and father had. He would assume that his own sons and grandsons could work there as well. So many graduates of my high school took jobs on the mass-production line at the nearby Harrison Radiator plant that we students liked to say our school had signed a labor contract with Harrison, a joke not so absurd when you consider how well the petty rules and generally numbing instruction at American schools prepare their graduates to function like androids. Yet, by now, anyone who remembers the joke must think of it nostalgically. Mass-production lines all over the country are increasingly run by actual robots—which decline to join the union, don't take lunch breaks, and never cuss out the foreman. If I had gone to work at the power plant, I eventually would have learned that the plant was closing and that I could have more than summers off.

Most of the plants and mills surrounding my childhood neighborhood have closed, moved, or downsized—Bethlehem Steel, Chevrolet Foundry, Killinger, Trico, National Gypsum, Buffalo Envelope, JH Williams, Fisher-Price, ConAgra Maple Leaf Milling, Nabisco, and many more—and in the meantime the politicians repeat mechanically, like the Chatty Cathy dolls manufactured by the Mattel corporation, the word *retraining*. The unions now plead: Please help us, Chatty Cathy. Because denied the opportunities and hazards of work for the company, how do men and women buy the supplies needed for adding on a bedroom for a new child? How do they live in their work?

Al built his own house. He built an addition to his daughter's home, a garage for my childhood family when my father was near death, and a storage shed for my wife and me, and would accept no money, not even for the supplies. He hummed a lot whenever he was constructing a building, although if something went wrong, he would mutter, as if the split board or bent nail were alive, "You son of a bitch."

During his retirement, Al asked whether I would let him "put a vacation place" on the land where I lived, the same property where my father had built his cabin two decades earlier, and of course I said yes. Every other week or so my uncle would drive seventy miles south of his home near Niagara Falls to spend several days in a row working on the old and run-down house trailer he had bought and moved to my property; remodeling the interior, reroofing, hanging gutters, replacing the plumbing, painting the interior and exterior, putting down new flooring, adding more insulation. The trailer was unshaded and he would take breaks inside where he kept a ceiling and floor fan whirring, kicking back sweaty and shirtless in a lounge chair to drink cold beer until he felt cool enough to go back outside to live in his work.

My father hired no help when he built his cabin. No excavator or cement truck arrived at his cabin site. We dug the footer with picks and shovels, shoulders and backs; the cement mixer was powered by a gasoline generator, fed with gravel shoveled from the box of the pickup, and watered by buckets hauled from the pond; he chiseled and laid up the stone for the fireplace. My wife and I moved into the cabin a decade after his death, and, a few years later, as I was replacing paneling, I discovered an inscription on the underlying block wall: "This cabin built by Jim Phillips in the Years of Our Lord 1966–1971." It appeared to have been written with a piece of charred firewood, the lettering and numbering as black as the power plant coal.

Quite a few men of my acquaintance are too damaged to go on working hard, their joints grinding or lungs wheezing after decades of labor. My friend Terry was a dairy farmer and logger, but at age sixty-four he finds it nearly impossible to walk—to limp—more than a hundred feet at a time and can no longer work in the barn or woods. Opioids help, sometimes. He owns a bulldozer and takes excavating jobs when he can get them, assuming his dozer is running or that he has enough money to buy the parts necessary to repair it. He complains little about the pain or his inability to earn money. He complains a lot that he can't work. Two years ago, when his dozer was running but no excavating jobs were available to him, he decided to build a pond on his land. He finished the job except for plugging the dike where the dozer had pushed out the excavated soil and stone, and the gap remains to this day, the pond but a three-acre hole in the ground thick with goldenrod and ragweed in summer and deep with snow in winter. Occasionally I ask him when he plans to finish it; he shrugs in reply or changes the subject. I suspect that he needs to know that always there is work yet to do. If he finishes the pond, then what?

I wonder if is it possible for my daughter and son, college graduates who are the children of teachers, to understand what work means to those who could not attend college. During his break following his first year of college, my son labored for his uncle's landscaping business, and one day, out in punishing summer heat, the college kid screwed up an assigned task. "What happened?" his uncle asked. "Don't they teach this in the Ivy League?"

Sometimes I forget what hard physical work is like, what it must have been like day in and day out for my working-class ancestors, and what it must be like for immigrants and others who now perform the hardest, dirtiest, and lowest-paying jobs that remain. Yet last winter, during my break from teaching, I cut fire-wood and managed to recall a little about work. I recalled what I was taught about woodcutting by my maternal grandfather, who was simultaneously a farmer and highway worker and who, when I was a teenager, took me to the woods with him. He showed me how to fell a tree; how to recognize a widow-maker; what to do if a tree hangs up on its way down; how to know whether a length of log should be cut into pieces from the under or top side; how to split a large chunk of wood by working my way around it, knocking off outer pieces, squaring the chunk before attacking the core. He explained what a "face cord" was and how to pile one—a four-foot-high by eight-foot-long stack of firewood, each end perfectly perpendicular to the ground—without using end posts.

Snow and mud prevented me from driving my pickup up the steep lane behind the house, where my children liked to sled be-fore they grew up and left home. I lugged chainsaw, ax, and peavey up to where I would begin thinning the stand of two hundred black locust I had planted when my wife and I were still childless. The split and stacked wood would dry all spring and summer and warm my home throughout the next autumn and winter. I pulled on muffs to protect my hearing from the eventual violence of the saw, and, head tilted back, nose whispered by snowflakes, I circled a bole, judging its lean and the wind direction and determining where the tree was most weighted with limbs. I set the choke and yanked the saw rope. It purred. It screamed. Steel teeth chewed a wedge into the trunk, the rakers spewing yellow sapwood, before I moved to the opposite side of the tree and made a cut through it inches above the triangular gap, thereby forming a hinge to prevent a ton of wood from rocketing backward off the stump and into my legs. The crown nodded, and I shut down the saw and hurried to put distance between the bole and me.

The tree creaked and whined. Through packed snow and the thick soles of my boots, I felt the collision of sky with ground and remembered in that instant what it was to be limned by work.

LAY OF THE LAND

In the lumpy region I call home, a study determined, to the surprise of few, that tooth disease is our most serious health problem. If you're working three low-paying jobs just to get by, as did one of my neighbors until he had a stroke while cutting his firewood, who has time for the dentist even if you do have the money? I knew one guy who had extracted all of his teeth himself, except for those punched or stomped out: he would sit against a smooth tree, usually a wide beech, and after sufficiently lowering a bottle of whiskey would clamp onto the gray aching tooth with channel pliers and yank.

Here in the Alleghenies of southwestern New York State, we have a thousand small worries that amount to a giant gnawing worry—like the new forest that has been swallowing pastures and cropland for sixty years now because family dairy farms can't compete with the corporate farms out West. If you walk into an abandoned farmhouse, you'll notice that the plumbing and wiring have been scavenged, often recently, probably sold to a scrap metal dealer by someone hard up for drug money. The roof and second floor sag and the outer walls tilt inward as if a giant mouth is slowly closing. House trailers now outnumber farm-houses, and yet a previous supervisor of my town argued that because the trailers can depress the value of surrounding real estate, the Town Board should ban trailers. Maybe he thought the working poor should just scamper up the mountains and move into hollow trees, but what happened instead was that the trailer dwellers—the janitors and sales clerks and receptionists and loggers and hospital aides and highway laborers and the line workers at the factories that had been cutting shifts, some of these folks limping on damaged hips or backs or knees—crowded into the next town meeting and heated the hall with so much angry hurt that I thought I might get to see the supervisor model an outfit of sticky feathers.

It can sometimes seem that the land is emptying of charity, as if we are chased by predators and must defend ourselves with sticks, stones, and our remaining teeth.

As I hike the Alleghenies, I happen upon the remains of homesteads. The collapsing shale and sandstone ring of a hand-dug well, a drywall cellar still holding back the earth where trees rise from the leafy floor, and a knurled and dead apple tree mossy in the shade of a young forest all suggest that a farm or any other business has the substance of an American dream. Active factories are disappearing almost as fast as the farms. A manufacturer of electrical components constructed a new plant on the outskirts of a small town near my home but abandoned it a few years after production began; set back from the highway on a large expanse of grass at the foot of a forested mountain, the cavernous plant is still vacant a decade later. Trees thrive, though. Drive Interstate 86 from Hornell to Jamestown during the lush months and you will see one of the more beautiful landscapes in the country. Some people crossing the state make a sixty-mile detour to take I-86 instead of the New York State Thruway, just

to view the steep mountains and hills and narrow, pastured valleys—in places you can believe you are driving along the coast of
a stormy green sea.

Yet trees and wildlife didn't always have it this good. Despite
the unwelcoming nature of the place—much of the soil is acid-
ic hardpan, and people up in Buffalo refer to this region as "the
snow belt"—80 percent of the land was cleared for farming by
1910, eight decades after the arrival of the first settlers. The white
pines, some of them 4 feet thick and over 150 feet tall, were the
first to be felled, and floated down the Allegheny River to mills
in Pittsburgh; then the hemlock for the tannin-rich bark. The
hardwoods were too heavy to float far and were chopped down
and burned for potash, crop seed sowed around the stumps until
the pioneers had time to dig and pull them out with the aid of
oxen. The wolves, mountain lions, bobcats, and bears were shot,
trapped, and poisoned; the whitetail deer—and the now extinct
eastern elk—were commoditized by market hunters. In his memoir *Pioneer Life*, Philip Tome recounts an 1823 trip in a bateau that
leaves to our imagination the natural beauty lining the Allegheny
as he and two other market hunters haul in seines glutted with
flopping fish and peer down the barrels of their flintlocks: Tome
limits his description to business, the profitable killing of thousands of fish and sixty-seven deer on a single trip. Before long, a
person was far more likely to encounter a hog than a deer in what
little woods remained. Yet today wildlife thrives and two-thirds
of the land is forested. There are even places where you can fancy
that the ax and saw were never invented.

In 1998, an eighty-two-year-old man drove here from
California to unearth a can of coins he had buried as a boy in a
farming community known as Little Ireland, about thirty miles
from where I now live. Charles Sheets learned that Little Ireland
has become a ghost town of stone foundations within the forest

of Allegany State Park. He entered the woods carrying a metal detector and shovel, and before he lost his bearings on land that was once cultivated, he must have recalled the whitewashed planks of his cramped rough home, his mother's meticulous vegetable garden, the laundry on the line, the boasting rooster and muttering hens, his father in the dusty distance striding behind a one-bottom plow and a draft horse circled by birds dipping to pluck up earthworms, the little boy with a shiny can of rattling coins.

More than one hundred rangers and police and volunteers searched the forest for a week before they found the body.

One might suppose the beautiful landscape that my neighbors and I share or the long and deep recession in our local economy would encourage kinship, a warm diffusion of the community values which supposedly exist in rural America. It hasn't always turned out that way. Two of my young neighbors have done prison time for getting wasted on booze and who knows what else, hot-wiring the pickup of the town justice, and setting it aflame at an abandoned county landfill. Could have inspired a heck of a Norman Rockwell painting: *Boys Roasting Weenies up at the Dump.*

Instead we're unified in our awe and fear of mountain lions. As we peer out at the increasingly wild land rolling through the decades and centuries, we perceive that, by God, a damn big mountain lion is out there. We're eating a fried breakfast or downing a beer after a shift at the cheese plant or changing the baby's diaper green with Gerber's peas when we spot it on the back hillside: a lanky and long-toothed and curve-clawed and man-eating feline that can leap nearly forty feet and run forty-five miles per hour. We quickly call in the pets, rush to the phone, spread the alarm to even the drunks and felons among us. The strange thing is that unlike the arsonists and foreclosing bankers, the big cats leave behind no sign. No tracks in the snow and zilch deer-kills, even though a mountain lion will take a deer every few days. And our lions never get hit by cars or captured by the automatic trail cameras which are now so ubiquitous that I look around before peeing in the woods—worried I'll end up on YouTube. What's more, state wildlife biologists assert that despite the many calls they receive about sightings, with each caller insisting on the veracity of his vision and making passionate avowals of sobriety, no mountain lion has roamed here for a century and a half.

Yet it's not that our lions are unreal or that there's some highly contagious insanity in these parts. It's just that, unlike the bald eagle and osprey and wild turkey and wood duck and black bear and bobcat and fisher and beaver and river otter and brook trout that have indeed returned to our loping forest and clearing waters, our mountain lions are not physical. Our lions are spirits: banshees haunting us from the past, warning of the future, yowling at now.

As Archibald MacLeish read it, "The map of America is a map of endlessness, of opening out, of forever and ever." I was reminded of the poet's cartography of an infinite and sacred nation when a neighbor bristled at the news that I had spent my weekend planting one thousand spruce seedlings on my land, the first of eight thousand conifers I would set out in five years. "All you people planting trees," the farmer barked, "soon there won't be anyplace left for farming." Yet American dreams of forever, our totemic notion that the New World graces us with eternal economic and cultural growth, can lift and dissipate like fog when I hike the land. I step over the stone-polishing freshwater spring that offers my drinking water as it did to Horace Guild, the pioneer who kept corporeal mountain lions at bay while he cleared what are now my forty acres with a double bit ax; cross the oily hard-road that until recent years was gravel; pass the overgrown foundation of the Mallory place, home to a pioneer family that would lose a son in the Civil War. And I make the long climb up Seward Hill, which was forest and then pasture and now—several wars later—is becoming forest again.

Resting against a lightning-burnt sugar maple that shaded heifers when the Seward family still farmed, I see, beneath the shaggy green of the glacier-sculpted mountains and hills, the winding valleys threaded black with narrow macadam roads and the house trailers and satellite dishes and junked cars winking in the sunlight and the splotched brown and gray of barns in various states of collapse. I can also see that I needn't have planted those spruce and fir on my acres. Plenty of native hardwoods have come up of their own accord, already choking the aliens. If I could rest long enough against the scarred maple, it would grow and heal around my flesh, sealing Rip Van Winkle in a mausoleum. In the bright breeze atop Seward Hill—even though I love the woods, even though my soul would dry up and blow away like an old leaf if I had to live in a city—I can sympathize with the hardscrabble farmer I angered by planting trees, as I do with the blue-collar workers who drive past closed factories and wonder if theirs will be next. Sometimes when I hike the conifer stand I planted in youth, each of my steps now in shade and a bit arthritic, I can understand why the Puritans believed the dim forest floor to be the haunt of the devil, the calls of lions and wolves to be demonic. And why to a lot of struggling Americans, trees are meant to be cut—not planted. With its twenty-three million acres of new forest on land abandoned by agriculture, the Northeast is now wilder than it was a century ago. Isn't that verdant fact a cause for celebration in a time of unprecedented worldwide environmental damage and destruction? Yes—but if the land your pioneer ancestor cleared tree by tree and your granddad and dad farmed by the sweat of their brows from sunrise to sunset is now home to the wolf-coyote hybrid known as the eastern coyote, the howling is seriously haunting.

And even worse is the feline yowling. People say the lions lie in wait out on a tree limb, tails twitching, and with long claws and glinting teeth spring down on their prey. A friend tells me he hears them calling to each other in the woods up beyond a little cemetery where the chiseled names of pioneers have been weathered clear off some of the gravestones, and that the sound causes the hair on the back of his neck to stand up. I've seen neither hide nor hair of a mountain lion, but last winter, snowshoeing up behind the house, I came upon the frozen and diminished carcass of a small deer. I could see from the tracks that three coyotes had caught it in an opening in the spruce stand the previous night, one of them probably clamping its jaws on the deer's neck as is their wont, strangling it. Can you imagine its terror as it suffocated in the snowy night? They eviscerated their kill, gulped down the liver and heart and lungs and left the stomach and intestines behind as they dragged the lightened carcass into thick cover, where they consumed all of the flesh except for that of one hindquarter. They finished eating their kill the next night, leaving a scattering of hair and disjointed bones and the hollow rib cage and the frozen gut pile that remained until it disintegrated with the spring thaw.

Lately, walking on my land, I find myself wondering as I pass the weathered rib cage: Do the unemployed of Detroit hear the sirens as howls? Do the foreclosed of California hear the pronouncements of bankers as yowls? Why did I seem to snort with mockery as I wrote about the boys who stole and burned the truck? What hungry rage caused them to destroy the hard-earned property of a good man and neighbor? What wild fear caused us to incarcerate one of them, hard-bitten almost since birth, for eight years, longer than some investment bankers and securities traders who stole the savings and retirements of thousands of Americans? Why did one of my kin—while receiving good care in a Buffalo hospital—become livid about proposals for national health insurance that would cover the less fortunate? It would make his taxes go up, he howled. He had earned his insurance through hard work, he snarled.

Have we become as hollowed of love as a gnawed rib cage?

As I settled here in the rural township of Ischua thirty-seven years ago, I came to know my neighbors a mile around. We spent many winter evenings together in wood-heated parlors, snow scratching at the windows, conversing about our families and jobs and other neighbors and hunting and the weather or whatever was on the television, but never about mountain lions. I don't mean to suggest that we ever resided on heaven's acres, that we didn't always have some hate and hardness and despair. A neighbor who had custody of his grandson regularly lashed the boy with profane vitriol that I could hear a quarter-mile away when they were outside. And I recall that each morning a farmwife with an icy spouse would wait in the woods at the lonely top of my road until the milk truck stopped so she could spend some time up in the warm cab before hiking back home through the woods and fields. But neighbors shared cups of flour; neighbors fed the livestock and poultry of other neighbors who managed to get away for a short vacation; neighbors looked in on the sick and elderly.

Now that the farms have been parceled and sold, I have several new neighbors I don't know, in part because I've never knocked on their doors to welcome them to this neck of the woods and in part because if I did they might wonder why I was bothering them and what I wanted from them. I don't even know the names and faces of some. I'm not sure why we're becoming a community of strangers, but I do sense that something in the greater civic and religious mood has been changing and drifting over even the most remote hills and hollows of America.

The wind didn't always blow in the direction it does today. Two decades ago, nearly thirty people gathered at the home of Francis Brown after he was imploded by a stroke. A few were his relatives but most were his neighbors, some who lived miles away, and we were there to provide firewood for his wife, May. Terry Hurlburt and I felled and limbed beech and ash, and with his green, coughing tractor he dragged the bolls from the forest into a weedy field near the house where men with chainsaws cut logs into eighteen-inch chunks or operated hydraulic splitters and swung wedges. Men and women heaved pieces damp with sap into a wood trailer and each time it was heaped full Terry pulled the load with his John Deere and dumped it on May's front yard where women and children were stacking a two-winter supply of warmth. At noon, we took a break to meet on the Swift farm, where at long folding tables borrowed from a church and set up in the yard below the Holsteins on a hillside pasture, we passed around cider, we broke bread.

The small prefabricated house where Francis and May lived is several hundred yards above mine on a gravelly bench, and just beyond the narrow backyard the land resumes its steep ascent into forest. On a clear, windless morning several weeks after the funeral, the eastern horizon spun into orange and the sun began to float, the maples crimson, a crunchy frost clutching the grass, and I saw that the lights were on in the house and knew she had risen at the time when she used to cook him breakfast. From her crumbling chimney rose a steamy offering of burnt wood.

CALVIN'S WAGER

He loves "the girls down here," my new neighbor said. By "down here" he meant the Allegheny foothills south of Buffalo, down on the map and down in the economic and social order. "Give great blow jobs—because, you know, they can't afford false teeth." He must have known from my manner of speech that I grew up somewhere else; it could have been my sisters he was deriding, and he did not strike me as someone who had ever been in a fistfight. He must have known also that I wasn't taking up his time only to welcome him to the neighborhood and comment on his good taste in top-of-the-line all-terrain vehicles, and so I soon got around to asking whether I could hunt deer on his new property.

He said he'd *think* about it. Beneath the rattling jaundiced leaves of an oak, I appraised him in return; his head rested on his body like a helium balloon that had seen better days. I couldn't think of any woman for miles around—edentulous or not—who might give him even a Protestant handshake. He glanced into the deep hollow that fell away from his long driveway and appeared alarmed by the caroming gunfire. "Hey," he said, in a hurry now, "it's been nice talking to you." The shot had come from farther off, but probably he believed poachers were on his land. He glanced away again and then shook my hand quickly.

That's a city hunter, for you.

Thirty years ago, "city hunter" was a grinning characterization of any nimrod who drove more than forty miles to get to these God-forsaken foothills of the Alleghenies, but back then most of them were factory workers who wanted to escape home and get drunk and blast the bejesus out of something, maybe a cow honestly mistaken for a world-class trophy deer. Now that many of the factories up in Buffalo and Rochester have been vacated and sold for scrap, and blue-collar workers are becoming as rare as brown bats that have survived the white-nose fungus, "city hunter" means the businessman who made a killing by shipping jobs to Asia and then bought the hills and hollows we local folk were once free to tramp. "City hunter" is now pure epithet, though only behind his back.

Because who would be so addled to curse one of God's elect face-to-face?

B ad teeth. Bestiality. I've heard all the jokes. Get some whiskey in me and I might tell you a bunch. Yet no matter how drunk you get me, I know only a few jokes about the "elect."

A poet friend of mine who lives several miles southwest of my place once threw a party for a Manhattan writer who was scheduled to give a reading at a local library that was awarded an arts grant for bringing culture to the hinterlands. Because the visiting writer was a committee member of the National Book Foundation, his appearance seemed numinous to us backwoods readers and scribblers who knew of the organization that sponsored the National Book Awards. Flush with wine at dusk, my friend and I slipped outside with the amiable guest of honor, and hiked up the road, conversing in the good nature of the landscape. Parallel to the macadam, a stream tumbled down the steps and slides of a shallow and stony ravine beneath a fenced slope where bison grew fat for slaughter. Above the pasture, the land steepened abruptly into hardwood forest, over which a thin haze was settling, a translucent nightcap. In the west, the sun was lolling low and seemed to bestow upon my literary companions a golden hue, an award of sweet dreams, and to someone who couldn't hear us we might have been mistaken for transcendentalists, for three communing figures in a painting by Thomas Cole.

Maybe my friend was feeling as insecure as I was while we entertained a member of the Manhattan literati. Whatever the case, our talk was far from expounding on the spiritual qualities of nature as we built a theological fence between us and the people who lived in the trailer park on the other end of the road. Never mind that some of my kin have dwelled in trailers, and that my friend is usually much more kind than I am, we joked like tipsy Brahmins about trucks with gun racks, and eventually, as we passed a tumbledown barn, began to regale our guest with an account of regional scandal that no doubt had inspired a Sunday sermon or two on the state of man. The visitor from the city heard from us that in what became known as "the pony-poker case," police had investigated a complaint from a local citizen by concealing a video camera in her barn. One of her neighbors was subsequently caught on tape with his pants down, and despite his heartfelt defense that the ponies had always enjoyed his attention, was arrested for trespass and cruelty to animals.

Well, just suppose a man with the passion but not the money for equestrian pursuits received a sign: suppose it was a layoff notice or a foreclosure of his diary farm or an egalitarian wink that a pony gave him from its side of the barbed wire, but whatever, he instantly understood his fate and that there was not a single goddamn thing he could do about it. Suppose he gave abandon-ment to degenerative enjoyment that did not and could not involve exclusive restaurants and sports cars while the Lord held him over the fire as if he were "a loathsome insect," as Jonathan Edwards had so evocatively phrased it. What good would counseling or probation or thirty days in the county hoosegow do if his dam-nation were preordained? What good mere human forgiveness? What good prayer and penance? What good another condescend-ing, pull-yourself-up-by-your-bootstraps sermon by a member of the elect? What good a reading by a committee member of the National Book Foundation?

Oh, Black Beauty, come to me.

Here where the per capita income and average life expec-tancy are among the lowest in New York State, the working poor didn't have health insurance worth a latex glove before the enactment of the Affordable Care Act, and yet a lot of those same people are opposed to government health care, at least in prin-ciple. Quick to offer help to each other, they would prefer none from the government nursemaid, and except in communities of cultural outsiders, such as the village of Alfred, home to two col-leges, they tend to vote Republican on Election Day. Some of my Democratic acquaintances say they don't understand why this is Republican country, or as one of them asked rhetorically, "What's wrong with these people who vote against their self-interest?"

Yet even my most liberal of acquaintances seem on some level to fear the possible truth of what many around here believe to be certain: that as Jimmy Carter once put it, "Life is not fair." Our Baptist-in-Chief was shrugging off the lack of opportuni-ty for women in an androcentric culture, but could just as well have been counseling stoicism in the face of any other social or economic injustice. Since there is no use in blaming the privileged for what the Maker mysteriously willed, and since it is dangerous to criticize Him, the social order must be deemed proper. Maybe that's why, when we're not expressing bafflement or compassion, some of us liberals, although politically correct in a dozen other ways, will occasionally see fit to tell jokes and stories involving the gun racks and bestiality of the damned people we think of as rednecks or bumpkins. Consider journalism professor Stephen G. Bloom's profile of Iowa voters, in the February 2012 *Atlantic*: "Whether a schizophrenic, economically-depressed, and some say, culturally-challenged state like Iowa should host the first grassroots referendum to determine who will be the next president isn't at issue," he sniffed. "It's been this way since 1972, and there are no signs that it's going to change. In a perfect world, no way would Iowa ever be considered representative of America, or even a small part of it. Iowa's not representative of much."

It is one thing to put up with damnation by our Maker and quite another to tolerate damnation by mortals, especially by the professors and journalists among them. So what's wrong with these people who vote against their self-interest? It might be that quite a few of them vote Republican for a measure of earthly revenge, deicide being impossible.

John Calvin asserted that the saved and damned coexist mostly undetectable as such within all strata of society, but few Americans have been willing to accept as trustworthy someone who was both a Frenchman and lawyer. In the New World, where the words "money" and "monolatry" long ago bumped "monotheism" from the dictionary of the average Christian, it has always been easy to tell the elect from the masses. Go ahead, Occupy Wall Street as long as you desire, freeze your reprobate ass to the floor of your leaky tent, get mugged even: just don't think God cares in the least, and if you do start feeling holy in your sleeping bag, flick on your flashlight and check out Luke 12:32: the saved "are a little flock." By definition, the elect includes all of the American one percent, who will beget a new and smaller and richer generation of Kennedys and Bushes, just as Our Lord has always intended; "election doth run through the loins of godly parents for the most part," Increase Mather observed.

As for the 99 percent, it will of course soon grow to 99.5 percent. How do you think those people get warm in their tents? And no doubt a fair number of their babies will be born with birth defects, and not only because of parental abuse of drugs and alcohol, but also because, as Saint Augustine noted, deformity bespeaks the inherent sinfulness of a newborn. Go to Google and type in "trailer trash" and you'll find a laugh-riot's worth of sites chock-full of incest jokes and lots of knee-slapping pictures of really ugly and really dopey and really sinful-looking poor people.

Calvin's spirit carries in the trade winds, but as Pope Pius IV wrote of the lawyer's theology, "The strength of that heretic consisted in this, that money never had the slightest charm for him." Not that Calvin was a blessed-be-the-poor theologian. He was a blessed-be-the-lucky theologian. It is within the pro bono framework of his lawyerly reasoning that predestination makes perfect sense. If there is one God and He is the omniscient and omnipotent and omnipresent Creator who exists outside of time, He planned your entire surprise party right down to who wins the apple-dunking contest. Only at the end of the party, after you are handed the envelope containing your going-away card and a Play-Heaven lottery ticket, can you learn whether the pony poker becomes the harp strummer. You might just as well look for signs of the future in the entrails of goats as for salvation in material status. And if, like the overwhelming majority of lottery tickets, yours isn't a winner, you can do neither a goddamn nor graceful thing about it; Calvin seemed to have little tolerance for the equivocations of Augustine, Aquinas, Luther, or any other theologian who toyed with the possibility that humans are both predestined and free. Calvin denied that Adam and Eve were free to eschew the forbidden fruit. The Lord who hardened the heart of Pharaoh also required the first couple to swallow poison, bequeathing to the generations of man little more than the empty freedom to theologize vainly or resignedly.

And yet Pius IV was not completely accurate in his assessment of Calvin. The Play-Heaven lottery ticket is so terrifying that even that coolly logical theologian flinched before he could scratch; in his way, even Calvin tried to buy salvation. If God has preordained a fatally ill infant to hell, a great leap of faith is necessary for anyone to characterize Him as beneficent, but reasonably enough, just in case His mind can be changed, Calvin made a wager with the currency of flattery at the high bench of the Lord. To wit, we mortals are unable to recognize and understand His supreme beneficence.

Early on the day of the party for the Manhattan writer, I drove to town to buy ingredients for the apple pie I would take to the festivities. I passed house trailers pressed between roads and steep hillsides; a remodeled chicken coop where a father and son dwelled; and an abandoned farmhouse rumored to be inhabited by alcoholics, the cellar walls disintegrating and holey, the clapboards rotted and gashed, a human form drifting like a shadow past a broken window, the roofing wigged with vinyl tarp. The pie was a hit, and late in the party, as I prepared to say good-bye, the guest of honor quietly made a joke about the people who live in the hills and hollows of my region. It was not a very good joke, or at least I can no longer recall much of it, but maybe I just didn't understand it. I laughed anyhow.

LOST IN STORYLAND

In a time when lost stories seemed rare, Aunt Laura was the first I knew who lost one. In the gin mills near my home, where these days I can hear any number of stories about lost stories, some people say they lost their stories to thieves—but nobody blamed theft back when Laura lost hers.

Before she blew out her back in a furniture factory and became addicted to opiates, Laura enjoyed telling my sister Kim and me—our sister April was not yet born—tales populated by witches, ogres, and brave children. Laura never wrote her creations, but dramatized them in her gravelly voice, her laughter at our reactions reminding me of the hoarse barking of seals in the Buffalo zoo. Gestating characters and coursing nicotine freed her mind, I suppose, from her dull duties in the factory, while, in the smoky somewhere else of a new story, the children—the little people—triumphed because they were clever and brave and remembered to say their bedtime prayers. I imagine also that just before the initial amp of pain, when she used her back rather than her legs to lift her assigned end of a wooden industrial product, an elusive finale distracted her.

She babysat once while my parents were at a New Year's Eve party. My sister and I fell asleep on the couch before the ball dropped on television, but Laura woke us in time and later distributed pots and spoons and joined our celebration in our dark front yard, ringing welcome to the unknown, inrushing years. We beckoned the dead as well. When we were inside again, the floor puddled by snowy boots, the grump next door telephoned to complain. Laura suggested he have a good stiff drink. He called again in the morning, waking my hungover father to complain, and Dad suggested he pound salt.

In the possession of drugs, Aunt Laura no longer told us stories. Her words became slurred, her speech parsimonious and labored, and, like one of the dangerous creatures in her tales or the chained dog up the road, she snarled at the approach of children. One afternoon, Mom and Dad took her and my sister Kim out to lunch while I helped her husband, Uncle Pete, search their Buffalo apartment for the pills she had obtained by traveling from doctor to doctor, pharmacy to pharmacy, and who knows where else. I had almost as much fun as when hunting for Easter jellybeans. We found varicolored stashes under carpeting and grates and in the nooks of the pantry. As my uncle poured out pills hidden under the liner of a cereal box, they rattled into the kitchen sink like a frozen, shattered rainbow. After a heart attack killed Pete, Laura moved in with each of her four brothers, one after another, wearing out each welcome by falling asleep while smoking. When she arrived at our house, my father made her promise not to smoke in bed and to allow Mom to hold and dispense the cigarettes and pills. Mom went through the suitcases, which must have been humiliating for both women, but Laura was accustomed to circumventing searches—and that night Mom discovered her asleep atop a smoldering mattress.

Laura eventually moved in with a sister out in Michigan and stayed there for many years. I wonder whether, with her fairy tales lost, she told her sister grown-up stories to which her brothers would have been deaf, applauding too loudly their own.

So of the family stories within my personal story, one of the few about women (and the longest) is about a storyteller aunt who worked outside the home and was childless. I sometimes suspect that my father—who once informed me that having children improves a woman "just like having puppies makes a dog better"—assigned me to join Pete in the drug bust with the intention of teaching me what becomes of a woman who attempts to live in the wrong kind of story.

I know legends about my great-grandfather Samuel Phillips, the blacksmith who emigrated to America from County Down in the North of Ireland; and about Samuel's father, a County Down dirt farmer; and one about Samuel's grandfather, a seafaring horse trader from Wales who fell in love with a woman in Ulster and stayed. As female lives slip by unmentioned, an agnatic figurehead mounts the prow of family lore. I can repeat dozens of tales about my grandfather Phillips, the iron worker in Buffalo, but can tell you little more of my grandmother Phillips than her surname and that her sons thought her the world's best cook.

I can tell you, though, that one afternoon, when I was nine years old, during the gray years when Grandma had dementia, Grandpa drove to my home to say she no longer knew him and had told him her husband was dead. Standing in our kitchen, he wept as if he had lost everything.

It is doubtful to me that my grandfather could have imagined women breaking into the stores of stories. Or "the ethnics"—as my father-in-law referred to people who had darker skin than his—busting in, filling sacks, departing with precious words.

To some Americans it is still unimaginable. Men complain that women talk too much. White people complain that black people are too boisterous. And Hispanics talk too fast.

My wife every so often insists on recalling when we returned from a date and found her father asleep in a running car parked in the family driveway on a cold night. Margaret's mother had thrown him out of the house. Recently, I interrupted the narrative: "Yeah. I know. I was there."

She told it again anyhow.

A recent study found that the death rate for white middle-aged Americans, especially in the working class, is increasing. Premature death from drug overdose and suicide were considered to be possible causes for the increase, but no definite conclusions were drawn. In an interview cited by *New York Times* columnist Paul Krugman, Angus Deaton, one of the authors of the study, noted an anthropologist's theory that white middle-aged Americans "have lost the narrative of their lives." A number of white working-class folk have subsequently suffered my questions about their reportedly lost "narrative"—typically while we are entertained by a sporting event on a TV mounted to a wall behind a bar—and usually it is the men who reply, in effect, *Lost it, my ass. It was ripped off.*

A family with brown skin has moved into what is called a neighborhood hereabouts—which is to say, within three miles of my rural home. I know a few people who have taken this change as evidence that our neighborhood is hopelessly lost. Our loose neighborhood has been the scene of two police raids on crude methamphetamine laboratories, but those occurred some years ago, when the population here was still entirely white and nobody thought we were yet hopelessly lost. Within the past fifteen years, several neighborhood white guys have done prison time for drug peddling, arson, theft, and other such criminal acts formerly assumed to be distant and urban in nature, and yet neighborhood introspection is too superficial to halt the spread of certain rumors about our new neighbors. Stories circle like the wagons in a Zane Grey fiction.

During the long 2016 campaign season, some candidates warned that immigrants are stealing both employment and the American story. Factories are replacing workers with robots and our government has made it easy for corporations to move jobs to countries with labor laws as scarce and lax as those in the American Gilded Age, but according to some of the scripts that traveled across teleprompters, the immigrant population is—along with excessive taxation and regulation of business—a major cause of unemployment. In these contemporary Jim Crow yarns, which are devoid of any intended irony, immigrants are shiftless and yet labor long hours for employers who pay starvation wages rather than hiring U.S. citizens and paying them well.

I am reminded of the laboring characters in legends that seasoned the fare at my childhood dinner table. Unless smeared with grease or ground with coal dust, none had dark skin. Next to none was female. When, at age eighteen, I took a summer job in the coal-fired power plant where my father was a welder, almost the entire labor force there was white despite the plant's proximity to a large African American population that had its own family histories, including stories about employment applications lost in white, white Buffalo blizzards.

In the blue-collar stories I heard following our mealtime prayers, work is sacred even when the Phillips legends are tragic. Falls at construction sites jar stories forever from the skulls of three ancestors; the ribs of another crumble with the errant swing of a fellow worker's sledgehammer; and trees crush two kin in logging accidents, leaving both men with permanent disabilities. Surely the wounded required pain medication, and yet the pills and medical bills go unmentioned except in the story about Laura. The living return to work: we men were to remember that for his faithfulness, all that he lost was restored to Job.

The power plant where my father worked has closed, but it seems that some things never change. A neighbor of mine took gentler and lower-paying employment after rupturing spinal discs while laying out steel forms for concrete while working for a construction company; another is on disability because a fringe benefit of his job in a chemical plant was asbestosis; and one is back to work after an industrial accident and a year filled with surgeries and physical therapy. I know a fifty-something guy who returns from construction work so sore that after switching off the ignition he flips open the cooler kept in his pickup truck, downs a can of beer and soon another, nudges the driver-side door with his left shoulder, stiffly shifts his left foot onto the running board, has one more beer, and only several minutes after this necessary homecoming ritual does he find it bearable to actually limp into his home.

On my way to town one day, driving by collapsing barns and hillside pastures abandoned to hawthorn, I heard a member of Congress propose a further lifting of the national retirement age. A news person was mechanically asking the usual questions of the important man, who was giving the usual greased replies, reminding me that—some years before and not far from my home—a silage chopper bit into a farmer, and that when he didn't appear for dinner, it was his wife who found what remained of him.

If you would, consider for another few moments the surprising appeal of the businessman who was elected President of the United States in November 2016. A callus on neither hand. Famous in part for humiliating workers on national TV by screaming with evident joy, "You're fired!" Declared bankruptcy four times while some minimally paid workers have held down three jobs concurrently. Would any hard-laboring and weather-beaten or dusty-lunged American hope for such a man to become president? It once would have been hard to imagine. Yet in diners and gin mills in town I encounter hard-bitten white men who identify with Donald Trump. And hard-bitten white women who do, too. His supporters say he won't tolerate uppity women and will wall out immigrants, and they accept his handout of a tale in which he fights for people like them—and I can't help but wonder how overwhelming must the hunger for a story become before anyone would swallow one like that.

Once upon a time, the poacher was a sympathetic figure in the lore of the Phillips family. As he sipped whiskey one night in our parlor, my father described his grandfather and great-grandfather's method of quietly poaching pheasants from estates in the North of Ireland. They soaked grain in poteen, spread the bait in a remote corner of a field, and eventually wrung the necks of the intoxicated and helpless birds before stuffing the carcasses into a sack. In another of Dad's stories, a well-to-do landowner in rural New York discovers that a teenage trapper is poaching muskrats on his property. He chases the boy onto the small farm where my grandfather lived in his retirement. My grandfather, who happens to be outside, fetches a pitchfork from his barn and intervenes, allowing the lad to escape and thereby beating the devil at his own game. Yet these days, when stories are told at my family and neighborhood gatherings, the poacher is somehow no longer one of us. As voices rise over the hot spitting of the grill and the icy clattering from the beer cooler, the poacher is now characterized as a threatening outsider: a job-seeking Mexican who snuck across the border, an African American who benefited from affirmative action, a woman in a profession formerly reserved for men. And each time the poacher appears in a new story, usually as the usurper of someone's American dream, I recall a certain day when I was in my thirties and a friend and I pursued poachers—actually ourselves—through a winter forest.

My friend wanted to show me the landscape around the farm owned by the family of a woman he was dating. We set off late on a March morning, the snow somewhat blinding in the sunlight. On the far side of cropland, where after spring plowing one might find knapped tools of Native Americans, we unstrapped and removed our snowshoes temporarily so we could pass over a barbed wire fence and into a maple woods. Snow fleas swirled like windblown dust over the whiteness. Here and there, covered buckets hung dented and askance from spiles. Sap drummed tin. Trudging onward, we shouldered our coats, and I was urged to be on alert for trespassers in the thickening forest beyond the sugar bush. "A lot of trouble with them around here," my friend explained. "Poaching deer."

Many bare trees and much bright snow later, he halted and lifted his right arm and hand into a droopy point. "Look—tracks. Poachers." The tracks resembled our own. Indignant at my suggestion that we were lost and had traveled the woods in a large circle, he said, "I know where I'm going."

So we set off after the two poachers, eyes watering in the glare, noses dripping, thighs and calves pushing off sorely and mechanically, snowshoes lifting and arcing, snow crunching under the rhythm of our march. His legs were longer than mine, and, eventually, laboring to match his pace, I caught one of my snowshoes on the other and tumbled face-first into the snow, righting myself only moments before he halted and pointed at new tracks.

"Damn," he said. "Now there are four of them."

AT LAST,
A FIGHTER'S PEACE

Honored with an award as "the best all-around student and athlete," Emanuel Fried graduated from Hutchinson High School in Buffalo during the Great Depression. One of his teachers found him a job at the DuPont Cellophane and Rayon factory, north of the city in a hazy string of manufacturing plants, refineries, and toxic dumps on the banks of the Niagara as it roiled wide and blue and sparkling and polluted toward Niagara Falls. Buffalo alumni of the University of Michigan awarded a scholarship to one graduate of Hutchinson each year, but with a job awaiting, Fried was little bothered that as a Jew he was unofficially ineligible for the scholarship. A job meant he could avoid hungering in breadlines, camping in Hooverville, or wandering and begging as a hobo.

In his 2010 memoir, *Most Dangerous Man*—written when he was 95 and published when 97—we see Fried dancing in the clouds at the DuPont plant before he became a labor organizer and actor and playwright and Communist target of the FBI. He was only beginning to become dangerous, reconnoitering with brio a place of rebellion, attempting to "ape the bravado" of the machine operators: "I would occasionally, while holding the handle of the wooden case with its bottles of samples of different chemical solutions I'd taken from the tanks, cockily leap back and forth from the catwalk on one machine to the catwalk on the next machine, though that was forbidden by management as being too dangerous." The operators, including the women who whistled at the handsome new guy during his first pass through the factory, did not seem to care that Marx and Engels had characterized each worker as "an appendage of the machine." Until you fall, a blue-collar job can seem like heaven.

On River Road, not far from the chemical plant where Fried had labored, my grandfather and father and uncle and I labored at various times in the coal-fired Niagara-Mohawk plant that produced electricity for western New York. Out in the coal yard, where several hundred thousand tons were kept in constant reserve, the fuel was gradually pushed to and fro to prevent it from erupting into flame under the pressure and heat of its immense weight. The shifting, black mountain dwarfed the growling bulldozers as if they were Chihuahuas nipping at the heels of a sluggish giant. The men on the dozers coughed. Inside the plant, there was more coughing. If you had a particularly dirty job, such as shoveling and sweeping fly ash and coal dust from the tops of boilers, you made periodic visits to the nurse to have your eyes swabbed with cotton that became black; and the gritty air was so hot and dry on the upper floors of the plant that if you didn't drink a large volume of water during a strenuous shift, you might not shit for a week.

I think of Fried leaping from catwalk to catwalk, cockily, absorbing the bravado that rose cool and misty from the machine operators below. I think of my father flipping down his welding helmet, snappily, the other workers averting their eyes as he plied his blinding trade. I think of his urgings that I become a teacher: "Imagine it, two weeks off for Christmas, another for Easter, every summer off. Every summer! Wear to work the same clothes you'll work in. Hands clean!" And yet I think of his once informing me, "You can tell if a man works just by shaking his hand, by feeling whether they're smooth or callused." Not what kind of work someone does, but if he works. I can't recall any time before that when we hugged or shook hands, but to demonstrate what he meant he took my hand to shake it. "You feel it?" He added, "And then there's the ones with hands soft as a baby's ass, but they squeeze yours hard. What does that tell you about them?" I suppose he meant that the toughest of men work with their hands, even though the big bosses and pencil pushers—and, yes, the teachers—were better paid.

When later I was a student at a teacher's college in Buffalo, I earned my tuition payments by working summers at the plant. My father said he could get me a full-time job there, but hoped I would finish college. I hated my time in the plant, and yet was tempted to go to work there for good: By July, I had a weight lifter's physique and enjoyed admiring myself in the bathroom mirror at home. My hands were callused from my many hours of shoveling up conveyor-spilled coal, and though coal dust had embedded within the hard, dead skin, its darkness displaced another with light whenever I rose at night and flipped the switch on my bedroom wall and again when I reached the bathroom. I knew that in its way my shoveling had helped to produce the light. My labor had helped keep in operation the plant that produced the electricity for our home and for every other at least fifty miles around; my skin and probably my lungs were becoming coal-dark, but in thousands of houses people could read by incandescent light, watch television, eat refrigerated food, shower with warm water, all thanks to the men in the plant. We power company employees knew it, though few other people ever gave us a thought.

On the other hand: summers off. Two weeks at Christmas! Another at Easter! If I did enough yard work during my teacher's summers off, would my hands become hard enough? I think of my father flipping open his lunchbox when the union was planning to strike, grinning, revealing a small part of some essential plant machinery he had sabotaged the day before the strike was scheduled to begin. I think of the time I asked whether he would change anything if he could live his life over. He replied quickly, firmly: "No." By then he was in his early forties and had been diagnosed with terminal prostate cancer, which had spread into his hips and spine, and in great pain he was still working at the plant with no intention of quitting as long as he had our family to support. I asked another question: Suppose the plant had caused his cancer, wouldn't he, if he had it to do over, go to college and try for a better job? Was I cruel or simply ignorant? I can't recall. I don't know. Maybe I don't wish to know.

"No," he said. "My best friends work at the plant."

At age ninety-five, distrusting himself, Emanuel Fried is in *Most Dangerous Man* unsure why he became a labor organizer. He wonders whether he was driven by hubris, by an urge to stand above rather than with anyone; whether his lifelong rebelliousness was hostility or righteousness; whether his marriage to a Buffalo artist whose parents were wealthy rendered him a gigolo; whether his failure to volunteer on behalf of the loyalist cause in the Spanish Civil War was cowardly. Even when the House Un-American Activities Committee targeted him, when organized labor rejected him as too dangerous, when the FBI harassed him and pressured employers to fire him, and when no mainstream theater in Buffalo would stage his plays that had been well received in New York City and Toronto, Fried still believed in his peaceful fight and his art, though eventually, when the Buffalo newspapers were identifying him as a Marxist public enemy and some of the community were ostracizing his wife and children, he began to wonder whether he was a selfish husband and father who had flattered himself into believing he was Prometheus. And he went on wondering for decades. Early in *Most Dangerous Man*, he explains, "I'd like to dig out, relentlessly and honestly—no matter what the cost to my ego—what were my true motivations beneath the surface of what I'd done with my life. It must seem silly, even stupid, to younger people, but at my advanced age I need to find out why I have become who I am—and who am I now?—in order to decide what to try to do with the rest of my life." Fried's 2010 memoir reminds me of Montaigne's telling us in "Why I Paint My Own Portrait," "What I offer here is not my teaching, but my study; not a lesson for others, but for myself."

Since in *Most Dangerous Man* Fried seems to have little interest in describing what he remembers, only in understanding it, a reader encounters few jump-off-the-page descriptions of labor struggles or factory workers or his gifted and disenchanted wife Rhonda. To experience any of those, you will need to read his plays *Drop Hammer* and *The Dodo Bird*; or his autobiographical novel, the *Un-American*; or his collection, *Meshugah and Other Stories*; or watch a recording of his one-man play about his marriage, *Boilermakers and Martinis*. In *Most Dangerous Man*, the light is inward.

Nor will you find much of a solid narrative thread. It's as if Fried and his readers are sitting around a kitchen table—after all, working-class people sit at kitchen tables when they discuss anything serious—or you are together at the watering hole a little south of Buffalo near Bethlehem Steel before the mill shut down and you each take a fresh egg from the bowl on the bar or table and crack the shell on the lip of your beer mug and release the innards to plop into the dark foam before you drink and reminisce and reflect on your lives. One of you might begin to talk about your childhood when your immigrant father was a struggling traveling salesman and be reminded to tell a story about your own children and then you might talk about their mother and a long labor strike that put a severe strain on your marriage and about a play in which you wrote about some of these things you are yakking about and exploring yet again over beer and eggs at the scrubbed kitchen table or polished bar. If the two of you already know the outline of each other's life, this is good conversation.

Somewhere in all of this meandering talk and wonderment, you recall when movie producer Eliza Kazan asked you to play a role in *Boomerang*. One of your union pals was in a Buffalo hospital recovering from the amputation of a leg and you visited him to say good-bye, explaining that what you really are is an actor rather than a union organizer. Your friend reached up from the bed and squeezed your forearm, his grip still strong, and said, "Don't you abandon us, you redheaded son-of-a-bitch! Don't you abandon us!"

You didn't; and a different obscure actor, Karl Malden, was given the role.

On February 25, 2011, Emanuel Fried died at age ninety-seven. During the decade before his death, commentaries full of admiration of his courage and art appeared occasionally in the Buffalo print and televised media. By then, he was no longer quite so dangerous, and although on the covers and title pages of his books his name was Emanuel Fried, in the media he was referred to as Manny Fried. The commentators and reviewers seemed sincere, but since the *Buffalo News* had been running editorials criticizing public employee unions for costing the city and state too much money in salaries and benefits, I wonder what the editorialists would have said about Fried if he had been active in the labor movement as, say, the president of a teacher's or police union. Still, on the Friday of his death, news outlets in Buffalo paid tribute to Manny Fried's art and bravery. Coincidentally, on February 26, a rally was held in downtown Niagara Square in support of Wisconsin workers whose governor was attempting to outlaw collective bargaining for public employees; among the signs and banners several were hung in memory of Fried.

The rally was sparsely attended.

BIGOTS I HAVE LOVED

None of us players spoke up or left the field in protest of the metaphorical lynching. Our high school varsity team was preparing to play a team with a black and very talented halfback, and our varsity coach had designated one of his runners to play the role of the enemy. From the opposite end of the field, where I was practicing with the junior varsity, I heard him—his nickname was Boomer—over the theatrical snarling of the varsity. "Get the nigger! Get the nigger!"

Boomer was a churchgoer. He was the only one of my high school teachers to contact me after my father died during my freshman year of college; he drove to my home, sat with my family at the kitchen table, and shared gently his sympathy. You can find his actual name on the wall of fame at my old high school.

It might be ungrateful of me to recall my old coach as I have, but when you've loved as many bigots as I have, knowing how to remember them can seem as hard as that dusty and cracked football field where he deafened us boys. Maybe I should let bygones be bygones. Some claim that Faulkner was mistaken and the past really is past, racism in contemporary America little more than a rusty whip handle unearthed at the site of a Mississippi plantation. I've heard that the election of our first African American president was irrefutable evidence that racism in the United States has been reduced to a group of feeble old men peering watery-eyed through holes in soiled and tattered white sheets. I've heard from white people that fear of racism is as irrational as fear of ghosts. It is hoped they learned otherwise when white supremacists, young and old, men and women, many openly armed, marched in Charlottesville in August 2017. I hope so, but I doubt it.

On my way home from work on election day in 2008, I stopped for a beer. The Irish bartender glanced at my Obama shirt and told a joke to the guy on the stool next to me. "Did you hear Obama is ahead?"

"No. Is he?"

"Don't worry—that will change when the white people get off work and vote."

I asked the same guy, loudly enough for the bartender to hear, "Do you know if they serve seven-course Irish dinners here?"

"A what?"

"You know—a six-pack and potato."

My wife is mostly Irish and I'm partly, but my retort by slur was bigotry all the same. I had added to the stupid hate sputtering like old grease on the grill in that establishment where a patron could scribble whatever he desired on a dollar bill before the bartender tacked it to the wall above the bottles of whiskey. Where George Washington gushed, "I like Boobies!" What's more, since that election day, I've bought beer at that business where I heard the racist joke, and it wouldn't be impolite of you to ask why. In my neck of the woods, that bar is one of the few with Guinness on tap, and I am a weak man, but the answer is also that some of my fellow Americans drink elbow to elbow there and—for me—climbing up on one of those stools can be like going home again.

The first racist joke I heard as a child was told by a neighbor boy who heard it from his father. In my backyard, the boy asked, "What did God say when he made the second nigger?" I still hear the birdy, quavering voice of my neighbor, who walked to church with me on Sunday mornings, as he finishes the joke by assuming the Word of the Lord. In the punch line, God does not remind us that He created all people in His image, let alone demand an end to laughter at hatred. There on the green grass of my childhood, He says, "Oops, burnt another one."

Although I've allowed myself to forget, surely I laughed: I was already fluent in the tongues of bigotry, though I never used the slur "dago" in the presence of my best friend, who was Italian.

After he led us in prayer, thanking Our Father for supper, my own father made occasional ethnic slurs while telling stories about his day at the power plant or commenting on some news he'd heard on the radio while driving home. Usually the slurs were uttered as if he were reporting the weather, but he was not so casual when race riots erupted in nearby Buffalo. He feared that the violence would spread to Pendleton, home to merely a few black families.

We once ventured twenty miles from home into Buffalo's inner city to cheer the Buffalo Bills, the blue-collar defending champs of the upstart American Football League. My father parked the car on the small, yellowed yard of a house on mostly boarded-up Jefferson Avenue, paid the owner a two-dollar fee, and marched us to the game among an influx of pale humanity watched—predatorily, I imagined—by blacks sitting on front steps and porches, whole families bemused at the sight of so many whites staring straight ahead with silly terror in their eyes as they hurried up the avenue of false promises. Ticket scalpers and hot dog vendors hawked at busy intersections, and when we reached crumbling War Memorial Stadium, or the Old Rockpile, as it was called in western New York, my father said, for the second time that afternoon, "We'll be lucky if our car isn't stripped when we get back."

Somehow my father and the rest of us whites worrying toward the stadium had come to the backward conclusion that blacks had a history of harming whites. He and I had given little thought to what it felt like for the two blacks who attended my school or the few who labored at the power plant, but now we feared being in the minority. Inside the decaying but thick walls of the stadium, things would be made right again: the coaches and quarterbacks and security guards would be white like most of the fans. Even a boy could sense that football was the way America worked: a hierarchy of owner and directors and coaches and stars right on down to the wounded, grunting, and anonymous offensive linemen on whose wide shoulder pads every touchdown rested. And yet even a boy could sense that our nation had two working classes: one inside and one outside the gates.

Until my grandfather took a new job in the power plant he had helped build, all of the Phillips men were disposable iron workers. In three separate accidents, my great-grandfather and two of his sons died on construction jobs. My grandfather broke two ribs and bruised a lung in another. My maternal grandfather broke a leg on a road construction job; two other kin survived crushing injuries on logging jobs; another lost two and one-half of his fingers in a machine shop. Nearly every iron worker in the family had a damaged back before he reached retirement age, and they were among the lucky ones. When their bodies were broken or lifeless, industry purchased new bodies. Helplessly, my father knew this. On a sidewalk in the small city of Lockport, several miles from our home in Pendleton we once passed a stranger in a grandiose suit and glittering watch and gleaming shoes. Dad spit on the concrete, and muttered, "You son of a bitch."

My father, his killed grandfather, and two killed uncles did put food on the table while they lived. They could have been limited to starvation wages or sent to the endless unemployment line; and weren't they forever reminded? Aren't we all, we who have jobs? On some level they must have sensed that the well-to-do in America had twisted the word "black" into a definition of those who are perceived as inferior—and that their own skin pigment was no guarantee they would always be perceived as white. When my great-grandfather emigrated, he carried with him a Northern Irish and Protestant heirloom of anti-Catholic bigotry. Three generations of Phillipses lived in an Irish neighborhood of South Buffalo, and on their way home from public school my father and uncles and their Protestant pals fought Catholic boys who were on their way home from parochial school. The Protestant Irish thought of the Catholic Irish as black. Both thought of Italians as black. The Protestant and Catholic Irish, together with the Italians, thought of African Americans as black as black could be. My grandfather referred to Catholics as "cat-lickers," though he married one who agreed to give up her faith. Before I met the woman I would marry, who has kept her faith, I had a vague suspicion that Catholics had tails and horns, a fear she has mostly dispelled.

In his *How the Irish Became White*, historian Noel Ignatiev could be referring to my kin when he notes of his depiction of oppressed eighteenth- and nineteenth-century Irish Americans, "I hope I have shown that they were as radical in spirit as anyone in their circumstances might be, but that their radical impulses were betrayed by their decision to sign aboard the hunt for the white whale," which, he adds, "in the end did not fetch them much in our Nantucket market."

During the hike to the Old Rockpile, Dad bought us lunch at a hamburger stand. On the sidewalk, he counted his change and realized that the black cashier had accidentally handed him a twenty-dollar bill rather than a five; he got back in line, corrected the mistake, and explained to me, "They would have taken it out of her pay." It was a warm day in autumn, and as usual he was wearing a dark shirt that hid the coal dust, the blackness flushing from his pores as he perspired.

My mother never used the racial epithets that were second nature to other adults in my family and neighborhood. I like to think she was too intelligent to be bigoted—as if bigotry is caused by stupidity, an assumption of mine which probably goes to show that I'm not nearly as smart as I like to suppose. She had graduated first in her high school class but didn't attend college, as she explained it to me when I was a teenager, "because back then college was just for rich girls who wanted to find richer husbands." She grew up with Native Americans. Her father's small, swampy farm edged within a half mile of the Tonawanda Indian Reservation, where, until he died in his eighties, one of her uncles lived with a Native American woman in a cabin with no indoor toilet. My mother's younger sister married a man from the reservation, and although my grandparents loved their half-Indian grandchildren, their complaints about "lazy Indians" were sometimes slung at their gainfully employed son-in-law, and they felt certain that "them Indians must have took it" whenever a possession disappeared from the farm. Until my maternal grandfather landed a job on a state road crew when he was in his forties, they were poor, but my grandparents could always visit the reservation to witness destitute poverty, to be assured that though they couldn't afford to buy more than a few pair of underwear for each of their daughters, they were white.

I was spending a weekend eighteen miles east of my home, on my maternal grandparents' farm near Akron, New York, when Charley Moses—the brother of Millie Moses, who was my grandmother's closest friend—killed himself in his and Millie's log cabin on the reservation. Millie telephoned my grandmother minutes after the rifle blast. Over the phone, my grandmother asked Millie, "Was he drunk?" I begged them to take me along, but my grandparents ordered me to stay behind as they hurried out to their old American Motors sedan.

Early the next morning they returned to the reservation to clean Millie's parlor, and I went fishing in the muddy creek that shaped the sinuous east and north boundaries of the farm. I returned to the yard hours later dragging a stringer of gasping and flopping bullheads and rock bass, tormented by a cloud of mosquitoes, and encountered my grandmother kneeling on the grass with her hands plunged in a pail of soapy, pink water. I asked what she was doing, and she replied, "Trying to get brains off these curtains." She held up a curtain, and said, "Whoever would have thought Charlie Moses had so much brains?"

W e danced to James Brown and Aretha Franklin and perhaps the sensual celebration shook us awake to the images and calls of truth arisen. By then it was 1970 and some of us paid attention when our American history teacher taught about slavery, the KKK, and racial segregation, and when he asked, "How come you don't see anyone except white kids in this class?" Some of us were appalled by the old news footage of police assaulting peaceful civil rights protesters with truncheons, torrents of water, snarling dogs, and Southern law, and were stirred by the brave, truthful poetry of Reverend King, though by then he had been assassinated by a white supremacist. When the school board banned Eldridge Cleaver's *Soul on Ice* from the library, a small group of us protested, not because we admired the author's murderous, misogynistic rage but because, we argued, the school was supposed to be educating us, and Cleaver was of the American reality.

Of course, none of us walked off the football field in protest: other players might have been granted our positions.

A be Lincoln and Stephen Douglas we weren't, but my father and I entered into a series of debates involving racial issues. At first we disagreed about the banning of *Soul on Ice*, but as in all serious discussions involving race in America, we soon found it necessary to abolish boundaries and time, to visit George Wallace as well as Eldridge Cleaver, South Boston as well as Birmingham, and Africa as well as Harlem. He never argued overtly that blacks were genetically inferior, but my father was opposed to court-ordered integration of schools and affirmative action and believed that African Americans had accumulated more rights and opportunities than had whites. My mother, who knew her socially defined and confined place, listened in silence to our debates, which began during supper and lasted for hours. He thought about our disagreements while at work and I at school, and each of us charged into the new evening armed with arguments we believed to be fresh and potent. Dad actually asked a black worker at the power plant for his opinion on the Black Panthers, and reported to me triumphantly, "He told me they're all crazy."

We debated for three or four evenings in a row and then, weary from arguments that seemed to be going nowhere but circular, gave it a rest. We mostly avoided each other until he came to me after two days of quiet and said, "You know, all the black and white stuff we talked about, some of it you were right. You still got a lot to learn in life, but some of it you were right."

I nodded and looked away, embarrassed and proud like a son who has realized that for once his father has not let him win at basketball, that he has actually beaten his flawed hero. Which only goes to show that my father was right about one thing: even though he never again used a racial epithet in my presence, I still had a lot to learn about hate and love.

He was slowly dying. Men seldom develop cancer of the prostate until at least age fifty, but some studies have reported that welders have an earlier and higher incidence. He had been diagnosed with prostate cancer at age forty, and because it had already spread into his bones where it was inoperable, a surgeon had removed my father's testicles to deprive the tumors of hormonal fuel. He continued to limp into the power plant to support his family. On the days when he was in too much pain to work despite the drugs, his fellow welders did his jobs and hid him in a storage room so the big bosses wouldn't know to fire him. He eventually found it impossible to climb the stairs to the second-floor time clock, and took an early retirement, which lasted several months.

Even days before his death, he still was unable to wear a white shirt.

POSITIVELY 16TH STREET

It's hard to find a good bigot.

Several years ago I drove thirty miles northeast of my home to visit the Most Holy Family Monastery, which the Southern Poverty Law Center, a national civil rights organization, lists as a hate group. On my way, I stopped to buy gas on an Indian reservation—a forested mountainside, the weedy tip of Cuba Lake, several cottages, and a single Seneca Nation of Indians flag—and soon was off the tiny reservation and passing American flags of homes that ringed the rest of the lake like excessive eyeliner, then farmhouses in a long glacial valley, and eventually house trailers wedged between abrupt hillsides and flexuous back roads. Flags and flowers made the cemeteries almost pretty on that Memorial Day weekend.

The living were happily greasing their hands at fundraiser chicken barbecues in the eye-blink towns, fingering merchandise at yard sales, buying jam and bread at Amish stands, drinking cold beer on porches, ambling and chatting on uneven sidewalks. It had been a long winter. Even the hardworking woman who operated the full-service pump back at the gas station seemed thankful to be outside in the warmth, despite the fumes. I drove with my window down and left forearm dangling in the sunshine and wind and against the hot sheet metal of the door—on my way to the monastery.

The Most Holy Family Monastery is overseen by siblings Frederick and Robert Dimond, who go by the names Brother Michael and Brother Peter and consider themselves to be Benedictines—although the institutional Roman Catholic Church does not—and among the few true worshippers of Jesus Christ. For people who think of themselves as monks, the Dimonds have little apparent liking for the humble harmony of chant, seeming to favor scratchy old tunes, refrains of which could be heard decades or centuries ago: in the Northern Irish sermons of Free Presbyterian minister Ian Paisley, the American radio broadcasts of Catholic priest Charles Coughlin, and in the Spanish decrees of Grand Inquisitor Tomás de Torquemada. The disquisitions and philippics on the monastery website "expose" or "reveal" that each of the last several popes has been actually a demonic "anti-pope"; Islam is "false religion"; Protestants will burn forever and ever in hell; illuminati and freemasons are taking over the Vatican; and Jews are taking over everything else. Although the fantasies of the brothers are far from original, I hoped foolishly for an enlightening answer to an old, sun-blanched question: Why are some people inspired to loath in the name of the Jewish speaker of the Beatitudes? I hoped the Dimonds might reveal the wellsprings of religious hate, if unintentionally, but neither responded to my email and phone messages.

So I set off in my car.

Around the monastery, which is located off a gravel road, the cropland was verdant with timothy and red clover or stubbled with corn stalks left from the autumn harvest, while in the woodlots the wild leeks were jaundiced and shriveling, their season ending in the deepening shade of sugar maples. Two small, plain residences, several outbuildings, and a large wooden cross comprised most of the compound, and other than mine I saw no vehicles or activity. The grass in the lawn was as high as the timothy in the fields. A residence window was open, but no one answered my knocking at doors.

As I departed without having met the Dimonds, I noticed a pair of satellite dishes at the monastery. Cradling the TV and Internet cultures, they looked lonely.

Two years later, I made another attempt to interview an old-time bigot with a modern echo chamber. I wrote to Karl Hand, the founder of a second western New York group on the Southern Poverty Law Center's list of the hateful, explaining that I would like to know what had inspired him to hold beliefs expressed on his website.

The Racial Nationalist Party of America (RNPA), which has a City of Lockport address, maintains that the Shoah was no more than a hoax perpetrated by Zionists, and reflects the burning fear, common in the gin mills of certain white neighborhoods, that the American soul is endangered by the growing population of brown-skinned people in the United States, a demographic trend that Hand refers to as "genocide" against whites. Hand attended Catholic school as a boy but might have napped through the lesson on loving his neighbor; the RNPA online store offers all manner of "white power" pamphlets and music, including a down-home belting out of "Kajun Ku Klux Klan."

In the weekly *Niagara Falls Reporter*, columnist Mike Hudson has warned that a newsletter distributed by the RNPA praises as a hero the executed terrorist and racist Timothy McVeigh—who grew up in a town between the close cities of Lockport and Niagara Falls—but Hudson added that the RNPA probably "exists only in the minds of no more than a few deluded individuals."

Yet it exists somewhere. My letter was returned. "The RNPA, as a matter of policy, does not grant interviews," Karl Hand had written in a margin. "We have no need of your publicity." I knew where his apartment was but decided against driving seventy miles north to knock on the door: Hand's "We" brought to my mind the buzz of the Royal We of Loneliness, the sound of a sole occupant of a hornet nest, best left just like that.

It turned out my next search was not intentionally for bigots and took me a mere twelve miles south of my home. Surprisingly, at least to me, the Most Holy Family and RNPA websites had inspired me to do something I had not in years, except to attend weddings, communions, confirmations, and funerals of friends, kin, or neighbors. I went to church. I went on a humid morning when the lilac and locust blooms had passed in Olean, a factory town on the Allegheny River, but someone who stood under a large basswood would hear so many honeybees it could seem the entire town was humming.

After the energetic service at the Rock of Revelation Church, where the preacher was African American, I watched closely the children who passed through the vestibule. I watched two teenage girls and a boy pause on the hot oily blacktop of the parking lot to talk with a gospel musician, each in Sunday finery, almost their entire lives ahead of them, then cross the red bricks of Griffin Street, following a woman who was digging through a purse for car keys, and then, as they shut doors and the engine fired and they began to ride away safely, I understood exactly what had brought me to the church, what I was seeking, who I was looking for—though as it turned out, I never exactly saw them there, those four little girls with almost their entire lives ahead of them. I was elsewhere and in a much later decade; not in Alabama, in Birmingham, in the 16th Street Baptist Church, in the minutes before the bomb went off in the Year of Our Lord 1963.

THE DEVIL
MADE THEM DO IT

From April 1985 to May 1988, the devil lived in a small town six miles east of my home. His stay there in Cuba, New York, went unmentioned in the Geraldo Rivera documentary, *Devil Worship: Exposing Satan's Underground*, that aired on NBC in October 1988; or by popular radio broadcaster Paul Harvey, who liked to warn about Satanists in America; or by the magazines *Redbook, Woman's Day, Christianity Today, People, Life, or Maclean's*, all of which reported allegations of grave-robbing, suicide-inducing devil worshippers during the 1980s. Perhaps the writers and producers considered it anticlimactic that finally the devil was driven rather easily from southwestern New York.

In the Gospel of Luke, Jesus says that Satan fell to earth "like lightning from heaven"—and the devil did seem to arrive electrically in Cuba, if through a man-made circuit. In April 1985, a kite touched a power line in the town, electrocuting the twenty-three-year-old flier. About two months later, a cousin of the accident victim, another young man, committed suicide by hanging. In May 1987, a sixteen-year-old male shot himself in the head, and in March 1988 another young man killed himself, also with a gun. Between the first and third suicide, an out-of-towner was discovered murdered in a car abandoned in Cuba, and a village pharmacist was indicted for fraud and the illegal sale of drugs. In those days, when opiate addiction had yet to possess small town America, suicide and murder and fraud and drug peddling were fairly unusual occurrences in Cuba, a village of about 1,500 people, surrounded by farmland and forested hills and where locals refer to their part of the Allegheny Plateau as "God's Country." In a way, it is unsurprising that as grief and fear settled like fog upon the community, the second and third suicides became clouded by rumor that a cult of devil worshippers had lured young people into signing a suicide pact, manipulating or harassing them into sacrificing their lives to Satan. The pact—"the list"—was said to be growing.

Among the names of devils and demons in scripture, literature, and legend are Prince of this World, Beelzebub, Belial, Old Hairy, Atoti, Hutgin, Lilith, Magog, Moloch, Raguhel, Zizimar, Lord of Lust, Old Horny, Father of Lies. The devil is said to have tempted Christians in the form of a cat, goat, crow, pig, and toad. The devil or demons have masqueraded as angels, and, according to sixteenth-century writer Thomas Cranmer, as Christ. More commonly they have taken human form, often as well-dressed, articulate, and handsome men. The devil can be detected by his limp stemming from his fall from heaven, but tends to remain steps ahead of most Christians. The devil can impregnate a Christian woman, and a newborn demon can resemble the parish priest. Although demons can be driven away or exorcised, they continue to multiply; sixteenth-century theologian Martinus Barrhaus computed their number to be 2,665,866,746,664.

Two similar theories were offered to explain the rumors and panic in Cuba, which according to psychologist George Ronan, "reached pathological proportions." Ronan was director of a mental health counseling center in southwestern New York during the devil scare. He believed the rumors were "a by-product of scapegoating." People in the community "knew it wasn't impossible for suicide to affect their own families and they distanced themselves by saying the victims were different, that they were devil worshippers." Father Meegan, a priest who spoke with me on the sidewalk of the Roman Catholic Church in Cuba, said, "Rumor and gossip are after-effects of evil. The people who started those stories were afraid of their own lack of faith. They were afraid the devil is stronger than God."

As the rumors multiplied and became more sensational, the town police chief and the superintendent of schools found it difficult to accomplish more during their workdays than to respond to calls from citizens who demanded to know what was being done about the Satanists. Callers believed that youths were carving satanic symbols into their skin, painting satanic messages on bridges and walls, chanting in graveyards, pouring blood over the gravestones of the suicide victims, performing satanic ceremonies on railroad beds, stealing dogs and cats for sacrifice, listening to satanic messages on heavy-metal records played backward, and plotting to kidnap and ritually murder a blonde, blue-eyed virgin girl.

Although during various historical periods witch-hunters believed the devil to be the author of philosophy, art, dance, poetry, and music, by 1987 his aesthetic taste had degenerated. His art had become the purposeful vandalizing of public places with graffiti and his music the screaming of heavy metal. In their 1988 book *Unholy Sacrifices of the New Age,* authors Paul deParrie and Mary Pride claimed that "the National Education Association, pro-suicide groups and rock musicians are banding together to promote death for teens." And if the allegations of Texe Marrs, who headed Living Truth Ministries in Texas were true, the devil had substituted quality of message for quantity, and any wall with youthful scrawlings might sport a satanic symbol or image, such as the circle, triangle, diamond, pentagram, and hexagram; or unicorns, mermaids, eyes, wheels, crystals, peace signs, rainbows, and suns. "A deadly and evil wind is viciously blowing with magnum force across America and the globe," warned Marrs in *Mystery Mark of the New Age,* published in 1988 by Crossway Books, an imprint of Good News Publishers.

After the third suicide, parents worried about who might be the next victim in Cuba. As a local mental health counselor, Linda Wells, recalled, "fairly benign behaviors" were suddenly perceived as satanic and suicidal, behaviors including "minor changes in mood, lying, rebelliousness, minor use of alcohol or drugs, ways of dressing, or interest in certain types of music." Young people shrugged off adult worries about moodiness and music, but some resorted to birthday sleuthing to predict who would be the next victim: if a peer's birthday fell around the anniversary of a suicide, the boy or girl was deemed at risk. Kids fashioned such stories, adults repeated them, and soon scores of children were believed to be suicidal members of a satanic cult, a phenomenon that followed the typical pattern of UFO sightings—one is rumored and shortly the heavens are full of metallic saucers piloted by little green beings. A state police commander in the region cautioned me, however, that UFO sightings and devil fantasies are in one respect significantly different. People who tell stories about dangerous Satanists "must have victims, some-one who can be named. Otherwise, the rumors won't spread. If you claim there are devil worshippers in your town, you have to be able to attach names to at least a couple of them."

In *The Contemporary Faces of Satan*, one of numerous books about Satanists in the 1980s—published by religious presses, by presses specializing in conspiracy theories, or by the authors themselves—Christian psychologist Rabitor-Ray M. Jurjevich, PhD, cataloged figures and instruments formerly or currently in the service of the devil. They included Bishop James Pike, Thomas Jefferson, humanists, hypnotists, materialists, leftists, secular-ists, feminists, Hollywood, the Unification Church, transcenden-tal meditation, Trotsky, Rasputin, Paul Tillich, Ayn Rand, Andy Warhol, Ben Franklin, Frederick the Great, Diderot, de Chardin, Bismarck, Hans Kung, Carlos Castaneda, Spinoza, Dewey, Marcuse, Schopenhauer, Voltaire, Sartre, Jerry Rubin, Eugene McCarthy, Freud, Fromm, Jung, Skinner, Maslow, Betty Friedan, Julian Huxley, Benjamin Spock, sex education, the Enlightenment, jogging, anarchists, cynics. And the ACLU, the National Lawyer's Guild, Darwinism, Zen, parapsychology, beatniks, hippies, drug addicts, Harvard, Columbia, Planned Parenthood, homosexuals, astrology, heretics, pagans. And Pope Sylvester II, Pope Alexander VI, Pope Julius II, Pope Leo V, Saint Jerome, Vatican Council II, and the World Council of Churches. And the Renaissance, gyp-sies, abortionists, the French Revolution, *Reader's Digest, Village Voice, The New York Times, Denver Post, Baltimore Sun,* P.T.A. *Magazine, Ulysses,* Beacon Press, Putnam's Sons, University Books, liberal media, the American Library Association, French publishing houses. And vegetarianism, Hinduism, revolutionaries, Gestalt therapy, acupuncture, freemasons, rebels, nonconformists, iconoclasts, health foods. And meditation, situational ethics, health education, the YMCA. And Sweden, Persia, Arabia, India, Aspen, Anaheim High School. And negativists. And psychopaths.

The chosen one might have enjoyed the attention, or at least at first. The rumors set this teenage boy's suicide for May 31, 1988. He tended to be a loner, and when other kids asked him about his allegedly impending death, he responded merely with a mysterious smile. Yet when questioned by school superintendent Mike O'Brien, the boy denied any satanic involvement or suicidal intent. Clutching a copy of *Helter Skelter*, he made the same denials to Loren Sweet, the chief of the Cuba Police Department. Against the wishes of his parents, probation authorities confined the boy to a Rochester detention center for several weeks of "observation"—in large part because of the rumors. Juvenile authorities determined he was no threat to himself or anyone else, and he did no harm after his release.

As May 31 neared, a new subplot developed. A shadowy figure had been present at the suicides, urging on the three victims. The new story resembled parts of *This Present Darkness*, a novel by Frank Peretti published in 1986 by Good News Publishers, with eventual sales of 500,000 copies; set in a small town nestled in mountains and under siege by satanic forces, Peretti's tale involves demons and devil worshippers who urge country folk to commit suicide:

> "Kill the girl," Rafar shouted to Madeline.
>
> Madeline drew out a horrible, crooked knife. She placed it gently in Sandy's hand. "These chains are the chains of life; they are a prison of evil, of the lying mind, of illusion! Free your true self! Join me!"

In new rumors in Cuba, the three suicides were murders by Satanists. Not urgings, but murders. Worried that I might believe his department had missed evidence of homicides, Chief Sweet showed me several police photographs. Of one, he said, "Look here. See the powder burns on the lips and in the mouth? Notice no bruising to the lips or around them. No damage to the teeth. The weapon wasn't forced into his mouth. He put it in himself. He shot himself."

How can a devil hunter identify a secret worshipper of the Beast? In much old legend, the devil is black, frequently a Moor; but recently he might have converted to Judaism. Texe Marrs includes the Star of David in his list of satanic symbols. Rabitor-Ray Jurjevich's list of evil groups and influences include the Talmud, Kabbala, pharisaic rabbis, Hellenistic Jews, Jewish psychology, Jewish nihilists, militant Jews, Jewish bankers, international bankers, and the Anti-Defamation League. For the *Journal of American Folklore*, Peter Rojcewicz has collected and summarized legends about investigators of UFO phenomena warned by swarthy men—who dressed in black and limped and reeked and cast paralyzing spells—to call off their research. And according to one such story the men in black threatened fascist groups whose members were concurrently harassed by agents of extraterrestrial Jews.

In junior-high grades at the Cuba school, some children talked obsessively about who on "the list" would die next. One girl took to wearing head-to-toe black to school every day and informed school personnel that she was a witch. "I became quite concerned," said Superintendent O'Brien, "that the rumors themselves might cause us to lose a child." As Suicide Day approached for the next child on the mythical list, O'Brien and his staff worked at calming the schoolchildren by explaining the nature and danger of rumor. Yet many of the children were already skeptical or insulted by reports of devil worshippers in their midst, and most were easy to reassure. Subduing rumors spread by adults was on the other hand "like fighting shadows." O'Brien traced new rumors by telephoning the sources, and usually the trail ended after the second or third call when an adult storyteller would say, "I can't remember who told me." O'Brien would say something like, "Well, obviously the story made little impact on you. I'm relieved to know you don't believe it." After he was informed that a certain hilltop was littered with the bones of sacrificed animals, he hiked to the crest and searched the boneless forest.

So compelling were the storytellers that Chief Sweet at first suspected that a satanic cult existed in Cuba, but eventually believed the actual threat to be a type of virtual reality, and, like O'Brien, he saw the need to expose as shape-shifting fog the sources of the rumors. After a call came in that thirteen cats had been sacrificed along railroad tracks at the edge of town, an officer of the Cuba Police Department hiked the tracks and found the decomposed remains of a single cat. After a call came in that a large group of Satanists was performing a black mass in the cemetery, officers found instead three pre-adolescent girls holding lighted candles and swapping ghost tales.

This writer must admit that when he began hearing the rumors, it was hard to disbelieve. And for a while I spread them. Margaret was pregnant with our first child and I with various worries that could be boiled down to a related pair: would I be a good enough father and into what kind of world were we bringing an innocent child? In a hardware store or barbershop or out on a sidewalk, a storyteller would lean in as if we were strangers brought together by a natural disaster, all around us the cold flood waters pressing in. On the face of each storyteller was a look I have come to know on loved ones who have shared the grim news that the X-ray or biopsy found cancer.

I wish I could say that it was superior common sense or learning that finally led me to become suspicious of the stories—but rather, it was my impression of the occasional storyteller who spoke with no air of dread or grief. I became suspicious because of those who grinned their tales. Who reminded me of why my wife had disliked her paternal grandfather. I asked about him during one of our premarital dates, and she said, "He's a bastard." I then asked what makes him a bastard, and she said, "Well, for example, he likes to scare babies. Goes up to them and makes himself sound as mean as can be in his Irish brogue. He'll say, 'You dir-ty wee *divil.*' And if the poor baby cries, he laughs like hell. When he did it to one of my little sisters, my mother chewed him a new asshole."

Thank God for tough and protective mothers. Two citizens, both of them mothers, decided to organize a community meeting in Cuba to cast light into the fog—before the arrival of May 31. Yet while they planned the meeting in Cuba, the devil slipped out of town for a time. He was sighted in the nearby towns of Angelica, Portville, and Olean, and to the south in Bradford, Pennsylvania, and in the west in Erie. In Portville, Satanists were said to be assaulting children in school lavatories, sacrificing animals, and plotting to sacrifice a blonde, blue-eyed virgin girl in a cemetery under a midnight full moon. Portville teenagers meanwhile were repeating a story that two siblings who had recently moved into the district with their family had been expelled from their previous school because of membership in a satanic cult, and although officials at Portville Central School tried to dispel the rumor, the newcomers found their new community to be less welcoming than they might have hoped. The devil rumors dissipated after two officers of the New York State Police staked out a Portville cemetery on the night when a virgin was to be sacrificed. Lt. McCole later told me, "A group of kids did show up around midnight, but they weren't in black clothing, had no long knives hanging from their sides, and they had along no screaming female. Just a few giggling ones."

In the small city of Olean, someone discovered a piece of blood-smeared paper hanging from a knife stabbed into the creosoted wood of a telephone pole. The message on the paper read, "You'll go through hell before you get to heaven blonde haired blue eyed virgin." Lt. James Tambash of the Olean Police Department mused, "I could imagine a couple of thirteen-year-olds standing back as people read the note, going *tee-hee-hee*." For a couple of weeks, teenagers told him of sacrificed animals and endangered virgins. And then the stories faded away.

Secretly worshipped by much of mankind, the devil will take over the created world, according to many fundamentalist interpreters of the Book of Revelation. God will send plagues to punish devil worshippers before Christ and his troops on horseback destroy the fallen angel, who will enter battle as the Dragon. And small skirmishes were already underway in the 1980s. Archbishop O'Connor of New York declared the movie *The Exorcist* to be "gruesomely authentic"; the logotype of the Cult Crime Impact Network, which published a newsletter for interested law enforcement officials, depicted Christ on horseback spearing the Dragon; a woman in Chicago exorcised Satan from her five-year-old daughter by drowning her.

In May 1988, at a town meeting attended by about 350 people in the fire hall in Cuba, police and school personnel assured the gathered that allegations of local Satanism had been thoroughly investigated and found to be unsubstantiated. Relatives of the suicide victims spoke publically about their grief stirred anew by the rumors. Clergy and professional counselors urged focus on the real problems facing youth in the community rather than on nebulous fears that would cause new problems. Students, farmers, loggers, factory workers, retirees, and parents spoke about addressing adolescent alienation, and some of the attendees there took steps toward forming a citizens group that would approach the struggles of children constructively and compassionately. The meeting lasted until late in the evening; and by then the devil had packed his bags and fled the region. "The lie is the specific evil which man has introduced into nature," Martin Buber wrote in 1955; and in the days following the fire hall meeting, it was hard to find anyone other than the chief of the Cuba Police Department who admitted to having ever believed that the rumors about Satanists might be true.

Only "they" spread the rumors.

Only "they" believed.

It was not until the year 2000 when I again heard mention of Satanists in Cuba. At the time, I was a youth worker at a nonprofit organization in Cuba and one of my supervisors was a man who was prone to believe and promote conspiracy theories; one of his favorites was that Bill Clinton had ordered the murder of presidential aide Vince Foster and that the FBI covered up the crime by pronouncing the death a suicide. One afternoon, my boss returned from lunch beaming. He was a short man who was practiced at puffing himself up, and, standing in the center of the office, puffed and delighted, he announced, "It's beginning again. It's starting up all over again." He stood waiting for one of us subordinates to speak, and finally one did dutifully inquire about what it was that was starting up all over again. He told us that he had just noticed an out-of-state license plate on a car parked in front of one of the pharmacies in town and that the car also bore a bumper sticker that identified the owner as a member of Wicca, an organization for witches. "So, I mean the devil worshippers—they're back." I responded in as respectful of a tone as I could muster that the devil worshippers couldn't be back since they had never been in town to begin with. Of course, he didn't agree. "Your trouble is you can't see what is right in front of your face," he said.

OUR TOWN

I can no longer think about my hometown of Pendleton, New York, without first remembering that it is where Timothy McVeigh grew up. And when he wasn't thinking about the mountain of rubble in Oklahoma City, the lives he ruined or ended, what hometown reveries soothed him in his cell as he awaited his execution? Maybe he recalled his father coming into their home after a long day on the mass-production line at the radiator plant, the gray plastic lunchbox rattling with silverware as the tired man opened it and lifted out vending-machine candy for his children. Maybe he recalled fun with neighborhood friends. Maybe a girl who never knew he loved her.

After I recall what McVeigh did in Oklahoma City, I am free to reminisce about our hometown. Only then can I remember neighborhood battles fought with plastic guns—*Blam! Blam! You're dead*!—and with snowballs and green apples and horse chestnuts and BBs. I remember my father's rattling lunchbox. I recall two brothers crying and cursing as they jabbed at and circled each other with gardening tools. A boy who patiently helped me with my math homework. A boy who beat up three others in quick succession. Boys gently patting my back when they learned my father was dying. A boy who liked to decapitate nestlings with his hands, crush toads beneath his sneakers, and douse cats with gasoline before setting them aflame. Sandlot games of the national pastime. A father who once punched unconscious his mouthy son. Girls and boys in graduation gowns, posing in front of flower beds as parents wiped eyes and blinked and studied the drying Polaroid film. Two other boys and me on our backs on a lawn late at night, stargazing, talking with wonderment about something and nothing.

I can't remember much about the girls in my childhood neighborhood. They tended to stay inside, where they felt protected, although it is doubtful they were all that much safer there. One afternoon when I was a sixth grader, my sister Kim and I left the school bus together with a boy Kim had been mocking on the way home, and the boy, who with his mother and siblings had moved in across the road from my home to live with his grandparents while his father was serving overseas in the military, and who had become my friend, punched one of her shoulders hard. She collapsed howling onto the roadside gravel. I proceeded to attack him with my fists, until his cries were louder than hers. When my father came home from work, I told him what had happened, proud of myself, and he told me that I had done the right thing. He then told Kim she should not have started trouble between boys and proceeded to strap her with his belt. I saw no irony in the strapping.

I also cannot remember any word spoken by my high school graduation speaker, who must have stuck to the standard script about the value of community and the need for the young to go forth and make the world an even better place. I'm sure I would have believed him except that I was lusting for a girl sitting ahead of me instead of recalling that when I was sixteen and at a beer bash—thrown by a boy whose parents were on vacation—three boys from the nearby town of Lockport made the mistake of crashing the party while wearing the varsity jackets of their school. Now I remember well that a tightly smiling Pendleton boy walked up to them and said hello and swung his fist. And the room hushed as the Lockport boys froze for a moment before one of them spit out a mouthful of red froth and teeth. And other Pendleton boys closed in on the out-of-towners. And a case of bowling trophies smashed down. And the host kneeled over the debris and moaned over and over: "My father's gonna kill me." During the graduation speech, I didn't recall the line of cars packed with angry boys from Lockport that stopped outside the party house, or our host staggering into the front yard carrying a loaded shotgun, his father's, sweeping it back and forth, screaming "Get the hell outta here!" until the caravan began to pull away.

During the speech—the corny jokes, the touching anecdotes, the communal urging—I lusted for the girl who didn't know I loved her. I recall her often. I recall learning she was periodically raped by her father and that a different girl I knew had been gang-raped by several fathers of kids we knew in Pendleton. During our twentieth high school reunion, a woman told me about these assaults; we stood with drinks in hand looking at each other without saying anything more until a third classmate joined us to talk warmly about old times in Pendleton, where the boys we grew up with attended church, played baseball, did most of their homework, and loved their mothers.

After a boy from our town murdered 168 people and seriously injured 600 others on April 19, 1995, *Time* reporter George J. Church described Pendleton as a blissful place, and added, "How Timothy McVeigh, coming from this background, could have evolved into an embittered right-wing loner is not easy to imagine."

Church was right about one thing: it takes imagination to suppose a boy from Pendleton could grow up to be a mass murderer.

Inspired by the Hardy Boys mystery series that I read and reread throughout my childhood, I occasionally sneaked out my bedroom window to search my neighborhood for evil to defeat. But I saw more or less the same scene in house after house, night after night: a man in a comfortable chair in a carpeted living room, his wife and two of his children on the sofa beneath a big framed print of mountains or a lake or the ocean, all watching television, and the man rubbing his eyes and yawning as Lawrence Welk introduced the Lennon Sisters, who sang sweetly into the living room. Not until 1995 could I connect anyone from my hometown with murder and, even then, I didn't recognize the killer, who had been a toddler when I left Pendleton for good. Yet when the news cameras panned the murderer's hometown, I did recognize Pendleton. I recognized the church where little Timothy had received First Communion. I recognized our high school and the buses glinting in the spring sunshine as a teacher told the press that McVeigh had been a quiet student of average ability. I pictured and still picture the yellow buses growling past the squat town hall and dusty baseball diamonds and into the neighborhoods where over the thick green lawns the flags flew at half-mast.

NOBODY'S HOME

As rain melts winter, the Allegheny rises against the concrete and steel that protects distant Pittsburgh from icy flooding while upstream the river backs over mud flats that, until the U.S. Army Corps of Engineers completed construction of the Kinzua Dam in 1965, were dry fertile lands inhabited by members of the Seneca Nation of Indians. The Allegheny Reservoir has drowned ten thousand acres of the Seneca Nation, but its swelling never quite touches the city of Salamanca, New York, where the majority of inhabitants are white.

Despite its racial demographic, 80 percent of Salamanca is located within the Seneca Nation, making it the only U.S. city built on a Native American reservation. The non-Seneca who live in Seneca territory have never owned the land under their homes; and in February 1991, when their ninety-nine-year leases with the Nation expired, the lessees were advised by the Nation that in its opinion they had no ownership of even the houses in which they lived. As new leases were negotiated, home mortgages became difficult to secure, construction of homes ceased, and the rate of business closings increased in Salamanca.

In Salamanca, it can be somewhat difficult to find very many non-Seneca who are much troubled that in 1960 the U.S. Army

Corps of Engineers—with authorization given long before by the U.S. Flood Control Act of 1938—began construction of the Kinzua Dam. Or that soon after his election President Kennedy broke his campaign promise to protect Native American lands throughout the United States: ask not what the country will do for you, but what it will do to you. Yet plenty of Salamancans remain disappointed that the U.S. government has not defended "the property rights" of white folks in the city, although—given the history of the Allegheny Reservoir—it's hard to avoid the irony of the word "rights" as applied by aggrieved renters of Seneca land.

When dam construction began in 1960, the Seneca Nation had already surrendered or sold most of its ancestral territories in federal treaties and State of New York and Commonwealth of Pennsylvania deals that it accepted in part because whatever payment it would gain could be used to provide sustenance and medical care to its largely impoverished people. And because members of the U.S. Congress regularly threatened the Nation with federal termination of its status as a tribal entity. The Nation did go to court to halt construction of the Kinzua Dam, but saw its case dismissed although the deliberate flooding of Seneca land would violate the Pickering Treaty of 1794, which pledged that the United States would never "claim this land, nor disturb the Seneca Nation."

As it filled for the first time, the Reservoir covered the best Seneca farmland and the sites of Seneca homes, Christian churches, and a longhouse. Before the water arrived, buildings were torched or bulldozed. Woodlots were logged, bulldozed, burned, or simply submerged. Three thousand dead were disinterred and reburied on higher grounds. The displaced living Seneca were offered new homes in two relocation communities separated by thirty miles, but some refused those homes and settled in other places, including in Salamanca.

Some say the Nation was foolish for insisting on its ownership of buildings in non-flooded Salamanca. The critics note that as businesses and families abandon the city, lease income shrinks for the Seneca people; and that crime associated with poverty and despair threatens all residents of the city, where median family income, at around $29,000, is $13,000 under the county-wide median. Of course, such a way of measuring right and wrong, beginning as it does with the tabulation of money, is the root of the problem in a tragedy much older than either the Allegheny Reservoir or the city of Salamanca.

In *Land of Our Ancestors*, a 1994 documentary directed by Allan Forbes and produced by the Seneca Nation, a member of the Nation says something he probably heard when he was too young to understand it fully, though he understood and felt it deeply by the time the film was produced. Probably his parents and grandparents heard the same when they were children—but who knows what man or woman first gave to the echo its voice? *The white man is greedy.*

The Seneca controlled a wide territory until the American Revolution, the war between the whites, when the tribe aligned with the British government, the devil they already knew. The Continental Army troops of generals Sullivan and Clinton overran Seneca territory, burning food sources and villages. After the war, white speculators began to buy land from a tribe of starving and diseased people. More Seneca land was lost to speculator fraud condoned by Congress. By 1842, the Seneca were confined mostly to three territories in western New York, on lands coveted, as all Native American land was or would be coveted, by whites.

Named for a Spanish aristocrat and railroad investor, Salamanca was once a railroad hub—the Erie Railroad, Buffalo Railroad, Baltimore and Ohio Railroad, and the Rochester and Pittsburgh Railway had facilities in the city—and rail companies, along with white individuals, had by 1860 leased considerable land from individual Seneca and the Nation itself in violation of the Indian Trade and Intercourse Act of 1790, which prohibits leasing of Native American land without consent of the federal government. Without legal authority, the New York State Legislature passed laws pronouncing the leases to be legal; and then, as courts were voiding such laws, the lessees began lobbying the U.S. Congress, which did have Constitutional authority to approve the leases. In 1875 Congress approved most of the leases and created six "congressional villages" on Seneca land—one of which was Salamanca. As the saying goes, business thrived.

Initially the 1875 leases were for five-year terms, but were later extended to twelve for lessees who made "improvements." If, say, a lessee logged a stand of old growth forest and built a house or paper mill, the land was considered improved and the lease extended without negotiation. Yet this was not enough to satisfy whites in Salamanca, and in 1892 Congress extended the twelve-year leases to ninety-nine years, so that until 1991 the non-Seneca in the city could lease variously sized parcels of land for sums ranging from one to four dollars per year. Even ninety-nine years could not satisfy Congressman Edward Vreeland, a Salamanca bank president: in 1902, he argued unsuccessfully in the U.S. House of Representatives that white residents of the city should be granted title to "their lands."

When 1990 rolled around, the ninety-nine-year lease was about to expire and it became clear that the Seneca Nation would

claim ownership of improvements in Salamanca. The attorney
for the Salamanca Indian Lease Authority, which represented
the lessees in negotiations for the 1991 lease renewal, wrote in a
memo to the Authority, "If reason can be attributable to Congress,
an attribute I am bold enough to suggest, then we must conclude
that Congress intended the white settler to ever remain." The attorney, David Franz, urged against any "sale of our birthright,"
but acknowledged that for once the white settler might not pre-
vail. "Lady and Gentlemen, I perceive we are being invited into a
whore house—and you all know what happens next."

The Lease Authority reached agreement with the Nation, but
several hundred non-Seneca then joined the Salamanca Coalition
of United Taxpayers (SCOUT), which maintained that, despite
the colorful language of Attorney Franz, he and others who had
negotiated on behalf of the lessees had not put up a good enough
fight. I interviewed Franz for an article I was writing in 1991, and,
of SCOUT, he said, "They keep expecting John Wayne to come
charging over the hill."

The taxpayer group was similarly disappointed with Representative Amo Houghton, a Republican whose Congressional
district included Salamanca. Houghton had helped guide into law
the Seneca Nation Settlement Act, which provided that the United States and the State of New York pay the Seneca Nation $60
million in reparations for the century loss of its lands, a relatively small amount if Stanford University economist Joseph Stiglitz
was correct in his calculation that the ninety-nine-year lease had
cost the Seneca Nation around $262 million in potential revenue.
Houghton held that the Settlement Act was fair to the Seneca
and, because it helped to settle the lease negotiations, was ben-
eficial to Salamancans unable to obtain home mortgages until
they obtained new leases. Yet as some SCOUT members saw it,
Houghton was benefiting Indians at the expense of whites—not

unlike the character played by John Wayne in *War of the Wild-cats*, who, when asked by Indians if they should grant a generous lease to a wildcat driller, replied, "I think you'd be suckers."

City officials had estimated that under the assessment stipulations of the new lease, the average leaser of land and house would pay about $180 annually to the Seneca Nation. Some of the lessees objected to the reasonable if higher rent, including the operator of a trailer court who was charging each of his tenants about $100 a month to park a mobile home on land he leased from the Nation. Yet on the whole, SCOUT had less objection to higher rents than to other aspects of the lease. Its members were unhappy that the new agreement was for back-to-back forty-year terms rather than another ninety-nine, and that the Nation could require lessees to maintain their homes. SCOUT believed the lease violated tenant rights provided under State landlord-tenant laws and left unresolved who actually owned improvements (the Seneca Nation position that it owned improvements was eventually affirmed by federal courts). A SCOUT pamphlet complained that for the lessees—for those that David Franz had characterized as "the white settler" who should "forever remain"—the lease agreement was "humbling and belittling."

In 1991, there were Salamancans who were beginning to confuse their city with a federal fort located on the Great Plains of the nineteenth century. One SCOUT leader was cautioning, or perhaps threatening, that city whites were stockpiling defensive weapons and would dynamite their homes before agreeing to sign new leases. SCOUT hired a Buffalo attorney, Jennifer Coleman, to represent several members in a suit against the Seneca Nation, the suit arguing among other points that the lease act of 1890 forced upon the Seneca Nation another ninety-nine-year term.

I would come away from a public meeting of SCOUT members with the impression that legal fees had been collected to fill an anachronistic war chest:

COLEMAN: [*After telling the crowd that SCOUT co-chair Joe Fluent might individually sue the Seneca Nation*] If Joe lives—

CROWD: [*Laughter and applause*]

COLEMAN: I don't want that in the paper. It was a slip of the tongue.

VOICE: [*From the crowd*] Tell it like it is!

Attorneys for the Nation filed for dismissal of the SCOUT case, arguing that as a sovereignty the Nation was immune from suit. A U.S. district judge and appeals panel agreed with the Seneca position. The Supreme Court refused to hear an appeal. A small number of Salamancans refused to sign the new leases regardless, and the Nation negotiated with them for several years before evicting fifteen illegals.

In June of 2017, I spent a day in Salamanca, some of it in the Seneca-Iroquois National Museum, some in the Wildwood Grill, and the rest in Salamanca City Court, small settings in a tale that began when Christopher Columbus sailed into what he thought was the Indian Ocean.

In the Wildwood Grill, I talked with two white Salamancans who had resigned themselves to the leases with the Seneca Nation, one of them characterizing the leases as "fair." A third remained pissed off about the lease twenty-six years after signing it, but he was a hopeful guy, as testified to by his red and white and blue cap embossed with the logo of the Buffalo Bills. "If we can find a way to get it to his attention," he said, "I think President Trump would help us." I asked him why he thought the president would care, and he explained, "He didn't back down when the Indians tried to stop the pipeline out West."

I'd been to the small museum twice before, but wanted to see the Robert Griffing paintings on temporary exhibit there, his evocations of unspoiled eighteenth-century forests and waters and of Native American encounters with British officials and colonial traders. The museum is funded in part from Allegheny Reservoir reparation payments from the federal government. In the museum store, one white visitor—moved to patronization by the exhibits he had just viewed—advised a clerk to cherish his Seneca heritage and bequeath it to his children. Repeatedly, loudly, he gushed, "Teach them the language."

In City Court, I listened to the mangling language of lawyers as they and the judge discussed charges, pleas, bail, probation, mandatory counseling, and jail. The cases included charges of drug possession, drunken driving, assault, and theft. Some of the accused wore the blank masks of alcoholics and drug addicts, as if they had slipped out of bed, stood with difficulty, shuffled to the front door where someone was knocking persistently, and opened it a crack to whisper, "Can't you see nobody's home?"

In July 2017, as I do once every few years, I took a canoe trip on the Allegheny Reservoir. Early on a clear morning with little or no wind, before the jet and water skiers were active, I set off slightly north of the New York and Pennsylvania line and paddled in an upstream direction between steep forested slopes— the Reservoir resembling a fiord and seeming to narrow as it followed the path of an ancient glacier into a distance where the sky and water and mountains melded. I meandered leisurely and sightsaw for several hours, put ashore, and headed for level ground in a mountain gap where I would pitch my tent. I later found a small stream with brook trout large enough to be worth eating, and caught several and broke their necks and eviscerated them and wrapped each in moss soaked with spring water, and then in the evening back at camp threaded sapling branches into the mouths and out the vents of my catches and roasted each trout over a wood fire built on a large flat stone, and with my lips and teeth peeled the skin and picked the soft and sweet flesh from the fine bones as if eating corn on the cob. When I was finished with my dinner, the forest darkening and birds calling from the tree canopy just as they did centuries ago, I lit a pipe and found my way down to the stony shoreline, the surface of the Reservoir calm and streaked pink by the sun about to roll down the backside of a mountain. I saw a motor boat barely moving, the two fishermen trolling, and waited to see if either would connect with a fish, although it turned out that one hooked nothing and the other a snag, most likely a submerged tree stump or the foundation of a vanished home.

APPLAUSE
FOR THE MAGI

Late in that very rainy autumn the citizens of the river city of Olean, New York, debated whether to permit a soup kitchen into their downtown business district on North Union Street. Out in the valley, the Allegheny River breached earthen dikes, and while the Red Cross helped rural residents made homeless by icy and muddy water, I attended a dry and slightly contentious public meeting about the soup kitchen. There I heard a woman ask how the kitchen was supposed to benefit downtown businesses. Perhaps because the meeting was held in a church, with Christmas near and with small waves lapping at the edges of town, I sensed in her equally plaintive and scornful query an old Christian thorn: So how on earth is Jesus supposed to help the economy?

The soup kitchen in question was known as the Warming House. Several blocks from downtown, it had served the poor until the building where it rented space was sold and the leases terminated. An Olean businessman offered the charity new rental space on North Union Street, as well as a $5,000 donation for renovation of the site, but most of his fellow Olean merchants objected to the purposed mingling of commerce and altruism on grounds that the poor would repel shoppers from downtown. Several downtown businesses were already struggling to stay solvent.

Some citizens considered the Warming House guests to be repugnant. "These people," a dentist complained in a letter published in the *Olean Times Herald*, "congregate for free food and give nothing in return. They have no responsibility and demonstrate their poor manners and lack of respect on a daily basis." About the rabble on the sidewalk fronting the Warming House, some of whom occasionally cursed and littered, he added, "In warm weather, it is a dirty disaster. At least with our long winters, it moves inside more."

Meanwhile, many other citizens took shelter from the rain to write letters in support of the kitchen.

I know someone who was shocked by the dentist's holiday season sentiments, but I suppose my acquaintance hadn't paid attention to the fiery radio sermons of Rush and Glenn, or teed up in the immanency of golden sunshine at the right country club on the right Sunday mornings. And no doubt my acquaintance was unfamiliar with the poverty cure peddled by former South Carolina Lieutenant Governor André Bauer, a direct moral descendant of the enterprising narrator of Jonathan Swift's "A Modest Proposal." On the 2010 gubernatorial campaign trail, Bauer said, "My grandmother was not a highly educated woman, but she told me as a small child to quit feeding stray animals. You know why? Because they breed. You're facilitating the problem if you give an animal or a person ample food supply. They will reproduce, especially ones that don't think too much further than that."

Mercifully, no southwestern New York politician from the School of Malthus offered a winsome plan to end regional poverty—and shortly before Christmas, by a vote of 4 to 2, the Olean Planning Board granted a permit for the soup kitchen to open in the downtown business district.

So why, five years later, did I still hear the austere woman who asked, "So how's a soup kitchen supposed to help business?"

In the dry warmth of the Baptist church, she sat quietly on the pew in front of me until a friar from St. Bonaventure University, which sponsors the soup kitchen and where I am employed as a tutor, finished the unpleasant task of explaining how guests of the Warming House would be made invisible or fleeting to mollify merchants who fretted that consumers on their way to the jewelry shop would rather not encounter any poor soul or devil dressed in rags. Guests would be prohibited from entering the kitchen from busy North Union, required to enter instead from an alleyway, where a vestibule would be built. Absolutely no loitering would be tolerated near the Warming House. Guests would be prohibited from leaving their bicycles on the sidewalk. And their wheelchairs. Although I heard no promise or request that the Warming House shades be kept tightly drawn lest an impressionable child peek inside and be lured into a life of freeloading, it was clear that the homeostasis of delicate consumers required environmental protection.

The friar had finished making the politically necessary promises when the lady in front of me stumped him by asking, in effect, how a soup kitchen could possibly feed the bank accounts of businesses. Several seconds passed before a bearded gentleman broke the bewildered silence by urging that the Warming House staff inculcate their guests with self-reliance.

A professor of philosophy then stood and compared blame and dislike and fear of the guests to historical Hindu attitudes toward the Untouchables in India.

In my seat on a back pew, I drifted off a while. It seemed I had listened to the same discussion for a long time, longer than possible. It seemed that the debate in Olean had endured since at least since 1841 when Ralph Waldo Emerson asked dismissively, in his seminal "Self-Reliance," "Are they *my* poor?"

It seemed, too, that the philosophy professor's Hindu analogy understated the problem: that though they might condemn the poor to starvation, the André Bauers of our land are comforted by the presence of poverty. In certain Hindu temples, it was supposed that an Untouchable could have a better, if reincarnated life, but there in a Christian church, as citizens discussed the pros and cons of charity in relation to the lodestone of the economy and light of business, I was reminded that to some Americans the poor are the hopelessly damned, orphaned in the mangers and ghettos by a mercantile god, condemned to spend this life in an economic netherworld, where—now and then mentioned by journalists, clergy, or other sentimentalists—the poor are evidence that the affluent are saved. Proof that a poor man is as likely to pass into heaven as a camel through the eye of a needle.

And what could possibly move the elect to love those whom such a god never would?

Yet three teenagers were moved, rising diffidently from a pew, coming forward haltingly to present to a university official a donation for the Warming House. They belonged to a community service club at Olean High School, and with dozens of other students had gathered pledges before spending a night in cardboard boxes on the school grounds to demonstrate their sympathy for the poor of the world. The appeal of their peculiar innocence and the goodwill of many in the community were such that the check, representing a portion of the money raised for local charity, was for $4,700. The applause had become persistent when the lady in front of me positioned her hands and, turning her head sharply right, paused with seeming reluctance, as if in one of her palms she cradled a small turd. Yet presently and delicately, she did it: she clapped for the three who brought gifts.

TERRIBLE BEAUTY

Lugged from creek bottoms to be chiseled and laid flat against the hillside, the stones held warmth well after sunset and made good places for prone stargazing, a pastime enjoyed by children before the era of computers and cell phones. I imagine a certain boy asking a friend if he knew which one was the North Star, and that after his friend said no, the boy pointed and said that your gaze should follow the outer edge of the Big Dipper from the bottom to top of the bowl and continue in that direction until reaching the first bright star. I imagine also that because of certain names chiseled into the stones and of the bones below, he added that there used to be men and women who would find their way north by following that same star, their Star of Bethlehem, while they were trailed by other men who possessed hounds, rope, shotguns, and white skin.

To find the stones you need to poke and kick at the hillside with your shoes, because the markers are now covered by sod. The other markers in the cemetery, more numerous and on the higher and fairly level ground, were cut from marble or granite rather than shale and are still exposed to the light. The higher dead are sometimes honored with flags and flowers.

Yankee Hill Road is subject to flash flooding where it pass-
es the cemetery, but each of the cemetery dead was given a dry
enough resting place. In that sense the dead are equal. At an al-
titude of two thousand feet, Yankee begins abruptly its two-mile
fall to the base of the cemetery, the terrain forested and sloping away from the shoulders in a snaky vee. More than once I've
helped drivers who lost control of their vehicles and ended up in
the stony ditches or dense woods along the road, and I also, brak-
ing too gently, my pickup rolling fast, have had several close calls
with deer and once a bear jaywalking on Yankee. In August 2003,
heavy rain filled the ditches and spilled into the road, muddy
water hastening and swelling as it fell, sweeping chunks of macadam past the cemetery and into the flatland center of a township with the Native American name of Ischua. When correctly
pronounced the name sounds like the lisping hiss of fast water:
Ish-oo-way. Luckily for the living who had mostly forgotten the
dead, none of the flooding reached even the lower graves, deliv-
ering to town no bones.

It was in the midst of a drought when Ischua resident Cliff
Lowe told me a story about the stones. He was by then retired,
but a lifetime ago, before he began earning his living variously as a fur trapper, truck driver, factory laborer, and electrician,
he wondered about the hillside stones from which he stargazed.
The chiseled names "sounded different." Around town, teenage
Cliff began to ask about the names. He first heard the story of
the stones from Theo Clayson, who was an occasional gravedig-
ger back before Cliff was born. Ischua had once included two
small settlements of African Americans, according to Clayson.
Both settlements were established on leased land near grist and
lumber mills on Ischua Creek, and the renters dwelled in wood-
en shacks. Some worked for the mills and most of the families,
like the Irish Catholics in English-occupied Ireland, cultivated

and largely subsisted on potatoes. Clayson didn't know when or why African Americans first settled in the town. Did they come north on the Underground Railroad, traveling against the currents of the Ohio and Allegheny, intending to eventually reach Buffalo by foot or horse and somehow cross the Niagara into Canada, and did they instead put down roots near Ischua Creek when mill owners, whether sympathetically or exploitatively, offered them work and a place to build? In other words, were they somewhat like immigrants who today find a dangerous way into the United States? Or had they labored on the crews that dug the Genesee Valley Canal through the region? Clayson didn't know, and either did Ray Chambers, another old-timer who told Cliff more or less the same story about vanished settlements of African Americans.

What Clayson knew first-hand is that because African Americans were denied burials in the higher, flatter portion of the cemetery, their graves needed to be dug into the hillside— "into" because the slope was so steep. The wooden caskets "were almost standing up" when covered by Clayson. He said that he dug graves often during a typhoid epidemic that decimated both African American communities early in the twentieth century, earning good money for those days, maybe more than some of the dead had touched during their entire lifetimes. After the epidemic, the surviving residents of the settlements dispersed, abandoning their homes. Where did the people go? Nobody knows.

Supposedly one of the settlements was located on now generally abandoned Baxter Mill Road. Locally the road is known as Suicide Hollow because, as I've been told by a couple of my neighbors, "some people committed suicide in there." No one has been able to tell me who or when, or how or why.

Five decades ago, when he was still a young man, Cliff periodically trapped and hunted in Suicide Hollow and can recall coming across punky boards and timbers, rusty pots, jars emerald with moss, and the humpy overgrown rows of a former potato field. Yet I can find no written record of a settlement there. In 1994, Sally Pettengill, town historian at the time, self-published a 289-page history of Ischua, but her book makes no mention of African Americans other than those passing anonymously through town on the Underground Railroad. I notice no name that is "different" in the cemetery records, but perhaps that is because no one with such a name was buried in the upper cemetery. I asked Rose Edwards, our current, enthusiastic town historian about Cliff's story, and although she can speak knowledgably for hours about local history, she had heard nothing about any African American community in Ischua. Yet she remembers the hillside gravestones, some of which were still exposed to the sun when she was a girl, and "always wondered why people were buried on such a steep place."

Edwards could tell me, though, that several years ago a man was remodeling a home in Ischua, built for a white doctor in the nineteenth century, and in one wall discovered an old photograph of "a black woman and some love poems." Nobody knows any longer why the photo and poems were hidden in a wall or who the woman was.

In addition to the little cemetery near the town center, seven others are located in the hills and hollows of Ischua. Among the graves are those of dozens of Civil War veterans. According to the Pettengill history of Ischua, 101 townsmen enlisted or were drafted to fight for the Union. One might wonder whether the twenty-four who died far from home, including six who suffered tremendously in Andersonville Prison, fought for the winning or

losing side. Confederate flags flew until recently on a few proper-
ties in my neck of the woods, as if in celebration, like the Trump
signs that were not taken down following the 2016 election, and
as if our history teachers lied about which general surrendered
at Appomattox. They flew until the national backlash against the
white supremacists that marched in Charlottesville in the summer of 2017, when suddenly the flags were gone.

The names of the Ischua pioneers, they who put up log cab-
ins, cleared wilderness with double-bit axes, sowed crops around
sap-bleeding stumps, and raised the boys who went off to die
for the Union, have largely vanished from local cemeteries, the
stones fallen or vandalized, the chiseling smoothed blank by
150 years of weather. And a century from now, when southwestern New York is no longer a region dominated by whites—
Godspeed—our names will seem "different," those of us yet to die
and be buried in Ischua. A way of life is passing with us. Most of
the barns have collapsed and many of the farmhouses will soon
follow to the ground. Forest grows where corn and oats once did,
and where sheep and cows grazed. In the more populous and
developed of the surrounding towns, small factories are rusting
in disuse and those that remain in production are like members
of an endangered species. One day some teenage boy or girl will
wonder, who were those buried people with the strange names?
Where did they come from and why? How did they live?

In February 2017 it was reported that a decade earlier, when she
was in her sixties, Carolyn Bryant admitted she had fabricated
the story of Emmett Till grabbing and harassing her in August
1955. A couple of days after the confession was first in the news,
I was on a barstool sitting next to a guy who said he was relieved

he could retire soon, both because of his bad knees and his fear that before long the knife plant would close. He felt bad for the younger guys. Between beers and trips to the urinal he started reminiscing about better times and then sang with modest talent two verses of a song by Mary Hopkins: *Those were the days, my friend / We thought they'd never end.* From a nearby table, a man and woman clapped, and now, in the sepia of my memory, I see the couple through a haze of stratified smoke, leaning over the small table, gray heads nearly touching, applauding, but that can't be right, because New York State no longer allows smoking in bars. On our stools, my new acquaintance and I continued to converse, and eventually, because I couldn't get out of my head a recently reprinted photo of a tortured and murdered boy, I brought up Bryant's confession. But the nice guy next to me didn't seem to know who Emmett Till was. That same evening, I asked two other people. One knew.

Maybe because I'm no longer so sure as I once was about what I know or believe, I have developed a habit—a sort of nervous tic—of asking people what they know and believe. I know many people who voted for our president, including some of my kin, and I ask them if they believe him when he says things such as that Mexico doesn't "send" its best people here, but sends rapists; crowds of Muslims cheered in New Jersey when the Twin Towers collapsed; he will "send" the Feds into Chicago to end its gang killings; and that far from being a killer, Vladimir Putin is a "good guy." Some say sure they do; some say not all of it; some say not really. And then some ask me, but what politician can we believe, what can we believe, can we believe anything any longer? I study them and I'm not sure whether they do or do not believe the things the president has said and whether they do or do not believe we can't believe anything. And who are we, we who can't believe anything any longer? I try to remember. I draw a blank.

On September 28, 2015, the Alleghenies rippled beneath a blood moon. Colored by the Rayleigh scattering of light during some lunar eclipses, blood moons are not extremely rare, but the one in September nonetheless caused a tide of anxiety in many fundamentalist Christians familiar with a Book of Joel prophesy: "the sun will turn into darkness, and the moon into blood, before the great and terrible day of the Lord comes." The popular ministers Mark Blitz and John Hagee had disseminated widely their theological conclusion that the blood moon of the 28th would be the Big One, as people out in California refer to the earthquake which might one day dump much of the West Coast into the Pacific. Hagee's book on the prophecy reached number four on the *New York Times* bestseller list, demonstrating anew that ambulance chasing is a lucrative business.

As the night of the blood moon approached, one of my neighbors, a Christian fundamentalist, became, well, apocalyptic. "Something terrible is gonna happen," he warned in his front yard. "Something really terrible." As if he had forgotten I was present, he began to pace the lawn.

I thought the scarlet moon beautiful even though, disconcertingly, it looked as if covered by a translucent, fragile membrane—calling to mind a blood blister on a healing injury or an imminent aneurysm. Beyond the cast of incandescent light from my home, I gazed into the sky from the dock of my pond, but I now wish I had traveled Yankee Hill Road, parked my pickup, climbed partway up the slope of the cemetery, and lay back over the site of a sod-covered gravestone polished centuries earlier by the unbroken flow of a creek. Maybe there, under breathtaking sky and above old bones, I would have felt hopeful since all of us exist beneath the same firmament and shall be reclaimed by the same earth, before which, in our brief lifetimes, we perhaps can come to relish our mutual humanity. Then again, I might have felt something terrible is gonna happen.

BRIEF
INTIMACIES

TIME ENOUGH
FOR A STORY

While she shoveled food at my family, I thought of asking her the question about time. "Gimme your plate," she said to my wispy wife, the big serving spoon ready with a heap of mashed potatoes. "You need more."

She would soon join my grandfather in death, but for six decades my grandmother fueled a man who was concurrently a woodcutter, highway laborer, and farmer. As she saw it, a less than ravenous appetite in an otherwise healthy person was a symptom of sinful indolence. Whenever she cooked on her six-burner, combination wood-propane stove, pot lids rattled and clunked with salvation and the kitchen windows fogged even in summer. Her Bible reading had taught her that people bear the punishment of Adam and Eve: life is short and full of hard work, and you must fortify those you love.

The question I wished to ask was in itself benign, but perhaps not if directed at a person marking time on her final calendar. "I'm no fool," she had said to my mother after informing the oncologist that she was refusing treatment. "I think them doctors just wanna make more money off me before I die."

She had not touched the little food on her own plate, but tossed onto mine a second leg of fried chicken while I finished the first. Instead of asking the question on my mind, I found myself remembering—as I did whenever she served chicken—a story she had once told me about a November morning when she was newly married.

In my grandmother's shaped and clutched remembrance, in a story I have repeated to my children, Hope and Gabriel, and maybe they will tell theirs, she and my grandfather's extended family were plucking chickens, soggy and still warm, before eviscerating and disjointing them and canning most of the meat in quart mason jars on their Akron, New York, farm. The killed were heaped on the ground near a shallow, cast-iron scalding kettle hung over a wood fire and from a chain looped and bolted around a low limb of oak on the edge of the barnyard. Gripping the orange, scaly legs with his gloved hands, my grandfather's brother Hank kneeled and quickly dipped two carcasses at a time in the roiling pink water, wings spreading wide below the truncated necks, the heated quills loosening from their moorings for easier plucking as steam plumed through the arthritic fingers of the big tree. Stronger than even the cloying odor of manure, the musky smell of feathers clung to the yard.

No one noticed why, but her niece, a child of three with a scarf tied beneath her chin, ran close to the kettle, giggled at something, and backed against the rusty curve of iron. She felt the heat and yelped and jumped and sat for a moment teetering on the low lip, the cast iron beginning to sway there over the coals, and then, before her father could get hold of her, fell in backward. The shouts and screams drowned out the long commotion from the hen house, and hands ripped at her clothing, pink water streaming into her boots and overflowing onto the muddy ground as she was held upright on unbearable legs and feet, too many burning hands tearing at saturated cloth and at each other in a steaming blur across the barnyard from the slimy red chopping block. The hospital couldn't save her.

"I don't think anybody ate a thing the rest of the day and most of the next," my grandmother said. "But we didn't give up chicken. I guess it's a good thing we didn't live on the sea and get our food that way. It's a good thing it wasn't lobster."

I waited to ask my question until indirectly she mentioned her doom. It was as if she attempted to sneak the reality onto the table somewhere between the many bowls and platters of food. I asked my question after she asked her own while holding up a slice of Swiss by a corner: "Worms make them holes, don't they?"

"Did it go by fast? The time?"

She nodded, dropping the slice back onto the platter. She had no appetite. "Oh, yes." The raised window glass yet steamy, she gazed through a cotton-plugged screen and past the bug zapper hanging from baling twine tied to a beam of the white front porch and on past the marigolds and petunias and pansies edging the curving length of gravel driveway, into a pastured distance that I didn't know like she did. Slightly, she smiled at whatever it was she saw. "It went like Grandfather ate a piece of apple pie."

When it was time for her guests to leave, still wrapped in the white apron she followed us out to the stoop. She kissed my son, who was asleep in my arms, then hugged my wife and me. Next she bent with a groan and kissed my daughter, who was tugging at Margaret's dress—as if the girl had heard quite enough about worms. My grandmother lifted her apron and smock, and took

Margaret's hand and placed it on her abdomen where the skin was splotchy with brown and lined and stretched tightly over the home of the globular tumor. "You feel that? Don't it feel like I'm pregnant?"

A long time has passed since that day on the farm when the hog and chicken yards were abandoned and overgrown with aster and thistle, and the pasture empty of cattle and becoming shaggy with saplings, but several years ago, as my daughter, then twenty-three years old, and I drank in an Irish pub in the East Village of Manhattan, I recalled that day with my grandmother. Hope was employed at the Penguin Group, a publishing company there in the city, and we were discussing some political news reported that day in the *Times*. As parents often are when they study their grown children, I was moved by banality; during a pause in our conversation about a bill before Congress, I wondered where the time had gone and felt overwhelmed by love. Or was it self-pity? I pictured my daughter, bluish pink and weakly squirming, placed in my arms for the first time, when none of the hair on my forearms was yet gray.

Before the doctor permitted me to watch the C-section, he had asked whether I could tolerate the sight of blood. I replied, "I've gutted deer."

"Alright. You can watch."

Now in the pub I was almost teary. I glanced down at my napkin. And as if my grandmother had risen from the dead to distract me from embarrassment, I suddenly recalled that after I had asked her about the passage of time, she had looked into the distance with curiosity, which was more or less what I had been doing on that barstool in the moment before I slipped off and landed in sentimentality.

Then something strange and surprising happened as I next glanced up at Hope: I pictured her as an old lady.

When I was a child, I enjoyed holding tissue paper out the open windows of speeding cars, watching it flap and disintegrate until it was gone like a faded ghost.

During the third decade of my life, I knew nothing about Einstein-Rosen bridges, also known as wormholes, through which, it has been theorized by some physicists, we could time travel if only the gravity would not crush us as we were pulled into the hole—which is like saying that if not for death, we might never die. And yet like most people, I tried when I could to correct the past and improve the future: when I was thirty, I donated a kidney to my sister Kim.

An infection set in several days after the surgery, and because Kim had been receiving anti-rejection drugs that suppressed her immune system, the infection grew stronger despite the antibiotics injected repeatedly into her already black-and-blue arms and legs. The doctors came to suspect that the source of the persistent and spreading infection might be the transplanted kidney, so they removed it and performed a dissection in the operating room before sending samples to a lab. A few days after the slicing of the donor kidney, the source of infection was located in a heart valve. On her final day of life, she said, "I'm sorry you gave your kidney for nothing."

"I needed to lose a pound anyhow."

Of course, I now wish I had said more; but it all happened so fast.

When eventually I read about wormholes, I was sure that the fanciful or hubristic physicists had it wrong. Crushed or not, we cannot time travel through a swallowing wormhole; it's the other way around: we gulp our future as quickly as my grandfather could make remembrance of an apple pie.

Here's a story my grandmother liked to tell at mealtimes, most often when a noodle dish had been served. She had been babysitting on the farm on a frigid evening when my parents were out, had given my younger sister April a scrubbing in the enameled, cast-iron tub, and had dried her vigorously with a fluffy towel until she was brightly pink. Like an elated drunk, the toddler ran from the bathroom and into the pantry, squealing and staggering toward the kitchen. My grandmother chased her, thumping on arthritic joints over the creaking floor, fearful that April would fall against the recently stoked stove that was crackling and popping, the damper wide open, the room faintly smoky. When she caught April near the refrigerator—the white door covered with birth and wedding announcements and obituaries cut from the *Lockport Union-Sun & Journal*, cleaning tips from *Better Homes and Gardens*, and a yellowed copy of the Lord's Prayer with a flowery border—she noticed a bit of something out of place. She said sharply, "Hold still now." She kneeled. She pinched with her right thumb and index finger and pulled carefully, then with her left, hand over hand until she had extracted nearly a foot of writhing tapeworm.

"What's wrong?" she would say to her gagging guests. "It was kind of a pretty thing."

On some mornings of the summer of 1968, when I was fifteen and neither of my sisters were yet old enough for high school, my father would wake from pleasant dreams. He would wake without pain, even zestfully, and minutes would pass before he would recall the sinuous malignancy in his spine and hips. But those mornings were unusual. It was as if wherever he was, the sun shone on his back, and his shadow taunted him as it walked ahead.

The previous summer he had begun building a small hunting cabin on land he had bought in the Alleghenies, seventy miles south of Pendleton. Now he was in a hurry to finish the job. On weekends he and I shingled the roof, sided the block walls with plywood, and installed a door and windows. In late July, during his vacation from his welding job at a power plant, we started work on the concrete floor. In August, when the floor had hardened, we began cutting and laying the fireplace stones. Whenever his pain became too severe for him to work, I cleaned and put away the tools and stayed with him until he fell asleep on a cot, drugged on Darvon. While he dozed, I trained for football season on dirt roads, dammed forest brooks with sticks and stones and clay, and lay in meadows with sunshine on my face.

The rains came.

The dams burst.

Several summers ago, I tore down the treehouse I had built for my children in the woods above our house on the land where my father had built his cabin. With rough-cut pine and hemlock purchased from an Amish mill, I had constructed the treehouse eight feet above ground between four white pines that grew almost square to each other; it had a trap door in the floor, four windows and a tarred roof. I should have used hemlock exclusively: the pine had become so punky from the years of weather that the structure was beyond salvation. My children were grown by then, but I had hoped that grandchildren might someday play there. As I leaned a ladder against a wall and then commenced destruction, I was in a rotten mood, though eventually the rhythm of the work restored my spirits. I decided to save the more solid boards for the construction of an outhouse: Margaret had long wanted a second bathroom.

That evening, when Margaret was not at home, I removed the framed photographs from their places on the walls of our living room, de-shrining the images of our grandparents and parents and siblings of various frozen ages; our babies and toddlers and teenagers; Margaret and me dark-haired and smooth-faced and immortal. I knew Margaret would notice as soon as she entered the house, and with apprehension and guilt, I practiced my defense aloud: "We need to live in the present."

All but one I stacked and sealed in a cardboard box that I carried into the attic. The man in the spared photograph had lived in County Down, in the North of Ireland. I wasn't yet able to shape the right story of the other images, the seeming cacophony of them, but this one, of my great-great grandfather, William Phillips—named for William of Orange—was different. His mouth is open as if he is catching his breath, and he squeezes the wooden handles of a horse-drawn, one-bottom plow, his hands and neck sheathed in dirt, arms and belly massive, skull bald, beard trimmed raggedly and brindled with gray. He wears a grimy long-sleeve undershirt and a grimy long-sleeve work shirt with the top four buttons undone, the left sleeve of the outer shirt ripped off at the shoulder and the right hanging from the shoulder by strings, and pants patched at both knees, and earth-battered leather boots. He seems to glare past the picture-machine as if at something bobbing on the stone-dissolving sea over which his eldest son had faded forever away.

I hung the photograph of William Phillips on a wall of the air-conditioned office at the college where I work—in the present.

Although neither of us realized we were in his final year, I asked my Uncle Al the same question I had asked my grandmother. That day had been rainy, but the night was clear, the moon full, the landscape splashed with milk. We were sitting in creaky aluminum lawn chairs on the small lawn, drinking beer from cans and listening to the stream cascade through the ravine below his house trailer and to the frogs in the pond just beyond the dirt road and the owls and nighthawks and coyotes in the distance. I smelled both the freshness of the rainwater still clinging to the grass and the dankness of the muddy places in the road.

Because my uncle tended to be reticent, often stubbornly so, I usually waited for him to speak first when we drank together. That night in 1993, it was quite a while before he did. Without a prompt from me, he eventually commented in a matter-of-fact tone that it was hard for him to believe fifty years had passed since he joined the army. The last I had heard him speak of his military service was shortly after President George H. Bush was awarded the Distinguished Service Medal by the American Legion in 1991; in response to the award, Al mailed back his Legion membership card, which he had cut in half, he told me, because he considered Bush's vice-president, Dan Quayle, to have been a draft dodger during the time of the Vietnam War. Al would die in 1994, before the election of our current president, a saber rattler granted five draft deferments.

"Went fast; huh?"

He nodded.

After a few more minutes during which we clutched and sipped from our cans, he began to talk, quietly at first, about the war—which I had never heard him do before, despite my occasional prodding over the years. As I listened I became amazed at how long he spoke. He told me that after the attack on Pearl

Harbor he enlisted even though he had a wife and baby daughter and—as a welder in a power plant, an essential industry—was eligible for a deferment. He was stationed in the States until the invasion of Normandy and then was shipped to Europe. He once surprised an enemy soldier in a partially collapsed trench, somehow stranded there as his German comrades retreated from an Allied attack. The German threw down his rifle and held his hands high and pled for his life—or at least that's what my uncle assumed he was hearing—and, under fire, Al had to make a rapid decision. It was not any time to be taking a prisoner, and he didn't like the idea of climbing into the hole to take the weapon or the thought of turning his back with the rifle still within reach of the German, and so as the other young man looked up into his eyes and begged with arms raised and shaking, Al pulled the trigger. He said, "I got sort of paid back later."

What he meant was that he too was left behind in the fog of battle, after he was shot through the wrist while sneaking up on a machine gun emplacement to toss in a grenade. Al and a wounded sergeant spent the night side by side in a forest the Germans were shelling, and the sergeant was wounded again during the night, by shrapnel. As they hobbled up a dirt road the next morning, they encountered a German tank whose driver seemed as lost as they. The machine-gunner opened fire on the two Americans fleeing into the woods. Al was spun and knocked to the ground. The shot had torn through his flak jacket and had merely grazed a rib. The tank moved on. Later that day, he and the sergeant encountered American troops and were eventually transported to a hospital in England for surgery. From there, Al was shipped to a Long Island hospital for convalescence. He wondered if he would make it when, somewhere between the continents, the hospital ship began launching depth charges. Either it had been a false alarm or one of the charges had destroyed a stalking submarine, because the ship continued unscathed. A train took him home to western New York. With his right arm still in a sling, he learned that while he had been sleeping on mud and snow in Europe, his wife had been sleeping with her boss at the insurance company where she worked.

In the chair on the moonlit lawn, he began to talk about bodies: frozen distorted bodies with arms raised as if to heaven; bodies bloated with stench; bodies with entrails feeding flies and rats and dogs; smiling bodiless heads; faces wreathed brightly white with sheets of maggots. After telling me about the body of a child, he stopped gazing into the distance. He looked at me and finished his story about chaos and deliverance, a story which he must have hoped would outlast him. He said, "I don't know why I lived. I don't know why for sure. But I lived for some reason."

I thought I knew what he meant, my uncle who built a garage for my family when my father was near death; who became like a father to me after mine died; who was my best man at my wedding; who spent little money on himself but loaned me a large sum so that Margaret and I could renovate and expand my father's little hunting cabin into a proper house when we lived there with no electricity or running water; who, after Margaret and I made seven monthly payments, would not let us repay the remainder of the loan; and who liked to drink beer with me, usually with little talk.

It also struck me that if he could, the German who had died in the trench would tell a very different story.

Quickly, I embraced my uncle's story before the other could get its hook into me. I said, "Yes." And then, his empty beer cans in a neat upright row like his completed story, mine tipped and scattered, we became numb and mute in the bright and babbling night.

SPRING

It has taken me most of my life to know I am dreamed. I finally understood on a predawn when I was between sleep and wakefulness, just as in late March the weather was inhaling winter and exhaling spring. I believed I heard surf climbing and breaking, but I couldn't see water or anything else; my odd half-dream gave me a vague and yet alarming sensation that *the earth was without form and void, and darkness was upon the face of the deep.* I opened my eyes to a faint radiance of snowy yard beyond the low window near my bed, and I knew I had confused my sleepy rhythmic breathing with sounds of water, and I knew the water was real.

Dreams of spring used to begin for me in January when storms beat snow into drifts against the cabin where my wife and I lived during our twenties; when in the chicken house freshly added water froze over in minutes; when trees made cracking sounds; when the wind swept snow from patches of lawn, exposing browned grass that in March or April would infuse with green. I dreamed of spring while life endured beneath pond ice, packed snow, and soil indurate, and also above—survived blue gelid winds while the sun skirted the horizon, ashamed. When down and wool failed to keep me warm, I wondered how the whitetail deer, snowed into their forest "yards," could survive the cold and lack of food; and of course, some did not. Yet I knew that in early May, does would birth wobbly-legged fawns carried to duration through winter. And if during January I pressed an ear to one of my bee hives and tapped with knuckles, probably a brief whirring buzz would inform me all was well, the colony clustered and alive. Jays, doves, sparrows, juncos, creepers, cardinals, and grosbeaks visited my feeder, but only the chickadees learned that when I visited my apiary I would insert a stick through the lower hive entrances to sweep away dead bees fallen onto the bottom board; the chickadees followed me from tree to tree as I made my way to the apiary, finally alighting on branches close to the hives with feathers puffed against the cold, and invited the neighbors to dinner, *dee dee dee dee deeee;* and when I was done with my coroner's work the flock twittered in for what I supposed was an avian delicacy. A groan—as if at my anthropomorphism—would call my attention to the skyward angular swaying branches of a maple, and yet I would feel hopeful, knowing that come spring the maple would fill to overflowing with faintly sweet sap.

Out here, everyone has a spring ritual. I suppose the same is true in cities, but I know less about such people than about chickadees. For some—suburbanites too, I've heard—the ritual involves taking down the storm windows and washing the car in sunshine. For others here, it is plowing the vegetable garden and turning wet soil to be warmed by the sudden brilliance; or letting the cows out to green pasture when the ground has become adequately firm; or the first day of fly-fishing, speckled trout rising to sip gnats from the film of streams. Inebriated with joy, we tend to overdo it, as attested to annually by thousands of frost wilted vegetable plants set out too early north of the Mason-Dixon line; by pulled jogging muscles gotten on cold mornings; or, later in the spring, by Margaret's first attempt at sun tanning, which always results in a sunburn.

Anticipation would mount in April when an afternoon warmed enough for the bees to make cleansing flights, the voiding outside the hive of fecal matter held all winter. I was awed by snow browned a hundred feet around the hives and delighted by knowledge that nectar was on its way. And eventually the longed-for day arrived as plants effloresced into dandelion embers and dogwood puffs and scarlet blankets of hillside maple. I would inspect my hives, eager to find combs full of the pearly white larva indicating a laying queen. Honeybees are so contently busy on fine spring days that it is difficult to provoke them into stinging, and I dallied, leisurely gauging stores of honey and pollen, replacing old deteriorated comb with new wax sheets of foundation, scrapping bottom boards clean of colony debris. I set on each hive a honey-super for the days in June and July when the field bees would gather a surplus of nectar from rainbows of locust and basswood and thimbleberry and bird's-foot and sumac and clover and hawkweed.

Yet I was impatient and longed for an even earlier spring ritual. Watching my bees make cleansing flights over a bright snowy landscape filled me with a need, as my maternal grandmother used to put it, "to thin the blood after winter." I discovered the right anticoagulant when I helped a friend with maple sugaring.

Only eighty years ago the boiling of sap was *the* spring ritual in much of the Northeast and some of the Midwest. Families produced their own maple cream, candy, sugar, and syrup, and enough extra to sell "to pay them damn taxes." The tradition was absorbed from Native Americans, who, each spring when the ruckus of the crow took on a certain tone, welcomed the season of *maple moon*. They traveled through deep snow to maple stands, collected the sap in bark buckets, and boiled it in hollowed logs by dropping in a succession of red-hot rocks. Maple sugar was a seasoning and maple "gum" an important food during winter. The early invaders from Europe, who needed a source of sweetening to supplement the honey they took from straw skeps, boiled sap in iron kettles suspended over open fires. Eventually cane sugar was grown in the South; maple wood became valuable for furniture, leading to the cutting of many old sugar bushes; and maple syrup became a luxury. By the time I started producing syrup, only three of us were boiling within five miles of my home; sixty or seventy years before that, a dozen families might have raised steam on the warm sunny mornings that follow the clear freezing nights of March and April, finishing each sugaring season by throwing a "sugaring off party" right out in the bush.

I produced merely ten or so gallons of syrup in a season, though ten required of me as much work as for a commercial operation to produce a hundred. I didn't have the capital to invest in modern equipment, and anyhow the fancy stuff would have deducted from my satisfaction. With plastic sap lines running between trunks like electric lines between poles, I would be denied the pleasure of hearing the initial drumming and subsequent *plunk plunk* of sap, and the physical pleasure of hauling sap in pails by hand when the snow was too deep for my 1965 Farmall tractor; with a reverse-osmosis machine stripping most of the water from sap, I would be denied the pleasure of long nights in a sugar shack of my construction, stoking the evaporator with logs I had cut, and the reading of steam-dampened books under the yellowish-bluish hiss of a Coleman lantern. When I went outside to pee in the dark, I witnessed my life rise in a cloud needled by distant suns.

The buds would swell after a succession of warm nights and turn the sap bitter ("buddy"). A robin would *tut-tut-tut*—and it was time to pull buckets, wash equipment, and hang roadside the spring announcement: SYRUP FOR SALE. After the sugaring season, I would catch up on newspaper reading, the news every bit as awful as now. Yet I felt almost immortal in that first spring of sugaring following my thirtieth birthday and despite my ill-fated donation the previous summer of a kidney to my sister Kim, who died without ever leaving the hospital. I knew the maples would grow, shed glory, nurture spring in winter. I felt that humans, too, had within the capacity for rebirth. Why else would we go on crying and laughing?

All the while that I told you how I felt during springs past, I was a little embarrassed—or maybe "buddy." I'm unsure whether the feeling stemmed from who I believed I was then, who I am now, or both.

When Margaret and I lived in the cabin, we canned vegetables and fruit we grew or gathered and the flesh of wild animals I killed, sawed our winter supply of firewood, bathed in pond water, collected our drinking water from a hillside spring, and chilled in our outhouse. I once proposed to a publisher a book advocating lifelong self-sufficiency, never mind that at the time Margaret was a public school teacher and I the director of a home for juvenile delinquents; the publisher responded that my proscription might appeal to certain young people but that older Americans would become exhausted just by thinking about such a way of life. I thought, *Old fart*. A few years later, Margaret was pregnant and informed me we required electricity, running water, and a septic tank. When I demurred, she said, "Okay—but you will be in charge of washing the diapers by hand."

We modernized.

I stopped producing maple syrup several years after the birth of our second child. I told myself it was because the kids required so much of my time, but in retrospect I understand that already my engine was beginning to lose compression. Even after I quit my job to become a full-time househusband, it was increasingly difficult to stay up all night boiling sap and then function adequately and in good cheer the next day. During many a morning in early spring, I told myself I would trudge through snow to the sugar bush and drill and tap to resume the production of syrup, and in summers that I would patch the leaky sugar shack, but I never carried through. The roof began to sag. In my fifth decade of life, I tore down the building, which by then was a slumped and punky eyesore amidst a lovely wood.

As I finished writing "a slumped and punky eyesore," my memory of the shack was joined by one unbidden—attached like a deer tick—of a man I encounter at the Olean YMCA where I swim when my pond is too cool. I occasionally pass him while he leans on his cane and drags himself bent into the locker room, one foot elevated inches higher than the other by an orthopedic shoe and turned sharply outward, progressing so incrementally over the floor that I have changed into my trunks before he has reached his locker. I'm relieved if I avoid seeing him naked. His skin is splotched blue and pink and gray and dappled with many scabs, his nose lumpy and purplish, his hair long and yellow and gray and combed straight back stiffly, his testicles swollen like overripe fruit and penis concealed by a great sagging flap of abdominal skin. I might notice him as he creeps past the swimming pool and snails into the therapy pool, others vacating the water before he is knee-deep. He sits on the submerged tile bench and slumbers. I've never witnessed him make eye contact with anyone. I have heard him speak only once. On the afternoon of his speaking he had long departed the therapy pool and was finally approaching his locker next to mine as I dressed following a shower; concerned that he couldn't navigate the tight space between the locker and me—and also that he might brush against me—I said, loudly because I supposed him hard of hearing, "Let me get out of your way."

He was keeping track of his footwork, and without looking up he said, "Oh, no, that's quite alright. I'll be just fine, thank you."

The spiles and buckets and sap pan I have given away, but the evaporator arch sits naked in the woods, cast iron rusting, fire bricks crumbling, all settling into the ground. I wish to give the arch to a neighbor who collects and sells scrap metal to supplement his wood-cutter's income, but my son has asked me to keep it. He has finished law school and is moving away to work for a firm in Wyoming, but says he'll be back in two years to start his own practice and a family and in his spare time build a new sugar shack and produce syrup while using the arch his old man used. He's a dreamer who hasn't yet noticed he is dreamed. He and my daughter can remember taking breaks from early spring sleighing to join me in the sugar shack and be warmed by the fire in the evaporator. They recall my pouring cups of hot syrup over snowdrifts, cooling it into a sort of taffy they ate on their way back to the sleighs and hillside where Gracie, our Brittany Spaniel, liked to snatch their hats as they slid downward squealing as if on a terrifying roller coaster. My daughter graduated college with a BA in American literature and Irish language and then with an MBA, and is now in Boston and in the employ of a corporation. I'm still surprised that a former literature major has become a business executive, even though much literary scholarship resembles accounting.

I don't believe that my son will be back; marriages of the past and future rarely last. The arch rusts and my daughter will have cause to draw from her bank of books.

Spring comes earlier than it used to, but during winter I still put ear to wood, tap with knuckles, and listen for the whirring of bees here in the white and gray of the northern Alleghenies. Centuries after swarming from the skeps of invasive Europeans and gradually colonizing the Americas from hollow tree to hollow tree (Thomas Jefferson reported that some Native Americans referred to honeybees as "the white man's fly") invasive honeybees are threatened by two species of invasive mites, as well as by invasive pesticides and invasive GMO crops. I've downsized my apiary to two colonies, and late last winter I found one lifeless and moldy. The other ruptured forth in April, mites be damned, worker bees hearsing away the victims of winter and returning with nectar and pollen for the nourishment of newly hatched larva. Close to the hive, I sat in a lawn chair, watching them come and go. I drank beer in sunny hosanna.

A decade ago, I found it necessary to enclose my apiary with electric fencing to ward off black bears. To a bear, an apiary is an all-you-can-eat buffet. A commercial beekeeper near here so hates them that he used to soak sponges in liquefied bacon grease and scatter them around his apiaries: grease is digestible, but sponge much less so, and any undigested sponge expands with liquid and forms an intestinal blockage. It seems antithetical that a man who enjoys laboring alongside wild creatures—honeybees are as content to dwell in hollow trees as in manmade hives—would condemn any wildlife to such an unnecessary, excruciating, and prolonged dying, but the beekeeper invested in electric fencing only after an officer of the State Environmental Police warned him that he could be prosecuted for crimes including cruelty to animals. Financial profit is as sacrosanct in the hinterlands as on Wall Street.

My region has become bear country again largely because the profitability of small scale farming has declined; the northeastern United States is now on the whole wilder than when Thoreau lived on Walden Pond. Yet in the age of globalization, all of creation lives and dies in the same parish. I encounter bears in woods and bogs where American chestnut is now absent and where American elm nears extirpation and white ash and American beech are in a die-off; where all species of hardwoods are in danger of being eaten alive by the Asian longhorned beetle, which has been found on the East Coast and lacks natural enemies on this continent; where both the northern leopard frog and brown bat are now rare. Each of these indigenous species is under attack by invasive species or diseases. Some of the invaders are abetted by climate change, another by-product of commerce. Because of habitat loss where migratory birds spend their winters, diminished song welcomes spring and fewer butterflies grace summer. Although fed by a reliably cold freshwater spring, my pond has become too warm for trout. These obvious and relatively recent environmental changes continue to stun me.

I am stunned too by the apparent blindness of people oblivious to the evidence that human greed and overpopulation and fossil fuels are incompatible with birds and bees and fish and forests. And the lasting of civilization. I feel myself helplessly acknowledging the strength of philosophical and scientific arguments that humans possess as much free will as did the invasive asteroid that fried and froze the dinosaurs. I'm at a loss to explain otherwise why so many of my fellow citizens, including quite a few voters who seem to love the woods and waters as much as I do, are eager to vote for politicians who do the bidding of the fossil-fuel industry. The climate-change apologists, our contemporary flat-earthers, might be right to say that global warming is natural, if not at all in the sense that they mean.

With the arrival of each new spring, I wonder how many more I may live to see. I also wonder how much earlier in the year my final spring will arrive and how it will look and sound and feel; it's one thing to know I must vanish from the world, and another to know I must vanish from a world itself fading. And yet though the fading of my life and alteration of the earth should poison me with nostalgia, my joy endures, my helpless springtime joy.

It comes to me in dreams.

I AM THE SIN-EATER

To chip a hole into that summer-baked soil required the thrusting of a digging bar, a repeated bending and straightening of my back, and when the iron tip struck a large stone and threw a spark and set my arm bones aflame, I nearly cursed my uncle Fred for dying. The job was mine because two decades earlier, when Fred was a septuagenarian, he requested that—should his mortality ever be confirmed—his ashes be covered within hugging distance of where two of his brothers are nominally buried behind my home. Fred was a World War Two veteran, a former construction worker and union member, an old-time working-class Democrat, a hard-ass and yet a sentimentalist, and seemed powerless to prevent his gaze from fixing on beautiful women.

I wrote "nominally buried" in the previous paragraph because nobody picked up my father's ashes from the crematorium; and although my father's brother Al had wanted his own ashes interred on my property, months after the burial ceremony, Al's daughter let me know she had substituted wood ash and that her dad's real ashes were buried in her backyard. Two small gravestones mark the nominal resting places of two brothers, nonetheless. The grave for the third brother might be the real thing.

Fred didn't want a formal funeral, but I doubt he would have objected to his down-home send-off that was attended by his children, grandchildren, great-grandchildren, a niece, and a nephew—as well as several neighbors from the trailer park where he had resided until his move into an assisted-living home. Present were none of the women from his four failed marriages, but only one was still living and she was in poor health; however, she did mail the ashes of her and Fred's cat to be buried together with his. Fred had named the cat Bad News.

In our final phone conversation, Fred told me he had almost married again, to a woman who lived on a different floor of the assisted living home. "I really, really liked this gal," he said. "And she had a lot of money." He had intended to travel to Niagara Falls with her and propose while out on the *Maid of the Mist*, the tour boat that churns to the feet of the cataracts. "I know this guy who is a pastor. Called him and he was gonna be waiting for us when we got off the boat. Marry us right there on the dock."

Before Fred could carry out his plan, she died.

In the minutes before his ashes were buried, his daughter and a granddaughter spoke about Fred's love of storytelling, women, and life. His trailer-park neighbors said he was loads of fun and would be missed. On many summer mornings they would rise to the sight of him already hoeing his garden, his neighbors reported, although by some nights he was so drunk they had to help him to his bed. "We had a lot of good times," said one. "And some bad ones, too."

Standing graveside and quiet for the time being, I was thankful for Fred's decades of kindness to me, and for our good conversations and mutual laughter, but I also recalled a few strongly disapproving stories my father and uncle Al had told me about their brother. I wondered if anyone else still knows those stories. And how much did I really know about any of the other people present? And what of ourselves can any of us outlive? In the shade of a broad maple that was small when I placed on the hillside the gravestone of my father forty years earlier, I looked upon faces and on each met a mystery framed by retreating trees and jagged horizon and ravenous ground.

My turn came. I spoke about an old and now abandoned Gaelic and English tradition of hiring a sin-eater to be present at the wake of a loved one who died with an endangered soul. After a chunk of bread and bowl of beer or wine were placed on the corpse, the sin-eater, normally someone desperate for a few coins, ate sacrificially of the offering, absorbing the sins of the dearly departed and thereby allowing the soul a possibility of heavenly immortality. With a can of beer in my right hand, I used my left to pull a torn piece of bread from my shirt pocket. I washed down the bread with Molson Canadian. "So, Fred, don't worry," I said. "I got you."

Each of the adults who were standing before the hole had already downed a beer or two that afternoon, on a day that had been inevitable even for the last of my six uncles—who, before his heart gave out, had survived military service in World War Two, a pair of bad car crashes, cancer, a stroke, and enough whiskey to make mash of three livers—but later I worried I had caused offense by drinking to the possibility that Fred possessed character flaws, and had compounded my insensitivity by making sacrilege of sacrament. I considered that perhaps I should have remained altogether quiet. Or have added that a man might do wrong in part because—in the seeming immensity of living—he occasionally attempts to make sacrament of sacrilege. And that what a sin-eater actually means by wetting the bread is please forgive that man for his transgressions.

And me for mine.

SOULS OF
HILLS AND HOLLOWS

Despite those summer nights when I wake to the searing of macadam, the tires of rehabilitated junkers skidding or spinning, weeks can pass without my noticing in daylight any of the memorials along the narrow roads near my home, most of the road names ending with Hollow or Hill. I am surprised when something attracts my attention to one of the crosses. I might stop to lower my driver's side window and look and listen because a rangy cur has paused from a cool and sunny jog to lift a hind leg, making a canine prayer as the coltsfoot blooms in a landscape still piebald with snow.

The crosses are homemade and white like most others in rural America, each one of thousands marking where someone, usually a young man, died when a rusty car or rattly pickup met a bole or rolled and caught fire. Newly painted or washed, they are brilliant under a cerulean sky, although only when the acoustics are perfect do they whisper a story or complain laconically about dogs. They never become banal and officious like those that hector from high spires. They never shout to be heard over the sound of the enormous flag that flies above a small town several miles from my home, adorning a pole that according to local pride is the tallest in the eastern United States, the red and white and blue cloth snapping and crackling like a windblown conflagration in the clouds. They stay in their lowly place as if they have all the time in the world. They chill in snowdrifts, and fade in the presence of wildflowers, and point to migrating flocks, and glisten with dog urine, here on this pierced earth where you might occasionally detect in the susurrus of seasons the words of a story.

One of the crosses marks where one of my neighbors died. He had been released from jail and maybe—I've heard rumors but have never asked the widow—was celebrating freedom on the night when he rolled his car a half mile up the road from the trailer he shared with his family. It's been about twenty years since then and the first cross has been replaced, but so far, the hard hat affixed to both crosses has weathered the years with merely some fading. When the foliage has thinned in autumn, the view from the memorial is inspiring, encouraging you to contemplate the distance where Farwell Gulch traces a stream between the hills of red and yellow and gold and in the farther distance cradles a shimmering oval where the water is slowed by beaver. When I was a young man, a different neighbor, who was about the age I am now and who I considered to be an old-timer told me that a farmer used to let his beef cattle range free in Farwell Gulch, and that one of the bulls charged "a city hunter," who dropped his shotgun in fright and flight and spent hours up in a tree. The old-timer said that when he was younger he liked to fish for brook trout in the Gulch, but for a time the city of Olean trucked its garbage fourteen miles and buried it on property where Olean operated a small airport uphill from the Farwell Creek headwaters and after that the stream ran red and oily and stinky with leachate and the beaver ponds collected the dead trout and no longer shimmered. The stream now runs clear, but none of the trout recovered. I've heard there is a timber rattler den on a south slope above the gulch, but have never found it; I've heard that during Prohibition bootleggers made moonshine in the Gulch and I think I found the remains of their still a short way upstream from a shale cliff gushing a freshwater spring. For years an elderly lawyer from Buffalo owned the lower portion of the Gulch and loved to discuss its history and beauty. He also owned a hazardous waste company, was arrested for burying barrels of toxic waste in the Gulch, and died in prison a decade or so after I had lunch with him in his vacation chalet at the foot of the Gulch, when he still could pass as a nice guy.

A little north of the old bootleg operation and illegal toxic dump and perhaps mythical rattlesnake den, State Route 16 intersects Hatch Hill Road, where memorials were put up for two young people who died in a crash. One of the crosses still stands. On the other side of the state highway is Ischua Creek and somewhere on the other side of the creek is the vacant stone foundation of a tavern that supposedly was a hideout for big-time bootleggers; supposedly Al Capone drank and whored there on occasion. I know less about the young people who died in the crash than I do about Capone, but for a few days after the accident, during my drive to and from work, I would see blood stains on the pavement until an employee of the New York State Department of Transportation sprayed them over with black paint.

Someone purchased, sawed, bolted, painted, and planted the lumber of crosses. To remember, someone marked the earth.

The township in which I live and where I contemplate crosses is named Ischua and is located within the Ischua Valley and on Ischua Creek. It is assumed that the name is an English version of a Seneca-Iroquois word, but no one is certain what the word was or meant. An old joke has it that when the town was a new settlement surrounded by wilderness, an intoxicated and lost traveler stopped at a log cabin near the current location of the Ischua Volunteer Fire Company and asked, "Ish-oo-way Olean?"—and thereby gave name to the future town of Ischua. Many of the roads in the town are named for nineteenth-century settlers, and attached to each was a story—for example, that the Hatch of Hatch Hill Road felled a million board feet of virgin pine, or that the Farwell of Farwell Road dammed Ischua Creek and built a sawmill—but by now most of the tales have been forgotten. Before the coming of the whites and their guns, diseases, alcohol, surveying equipment, axes, plows, and dams, the Seneca memorialized the landscape by attaching stories to its features, navigating the wilderness by listening to stories that in time seemed to be spoken by the land itself, and were surprised when the white invaders claimed that living land could be owned. And yet, it must be noted here, the Seneca occasionally went to war with other Native Americans over territory. They lost their war with the whites and today most of the Seneca stories are too quiet to hear. The pioneer stories are fading as well as the old homesteads are carved up for suburbanites and city folk looking for vacation, hunting, or retirement property.

On my way to my job at St. Bonaventure University, I pass from Ischua into the town of Hinsdale, into the town of Olean and city of Olean, and finally into the town of Allegany. On mornings when I have paid attention to the roadside crosses I find myself wondering why the town and city lines were established where they are, and whether, regardless of the stories we tell, any boundary is real other than the temporary one we've created between humans and what we term "nature," "the natural world," "wilderness," "the wild," "the woods," "the bush," "the boundless sea."

The college that employs me is studded with crosses high and low, but as far as I know none marks the site of a car crash. The campus is normally a safe place, though several years ago the campus security office issued a midday email warning that students and employees should avoid the soccer field, where a bear was taking an afternoon nap. I went out into a parking lot where I could view our harmless visitor, but my attention soon shifted—as often happens when I am on a sidewalk or parking lot—to markers of more distant stories. In this instance, I was called to a hillside story.

Beyond the black and sun-soaked hump near the goal line, the Allegheny River washed the feet of hills, and, high on a sloping thigh above the river, forest enfolded a heart-shaped clearing called Merton's Heart, after the writer Thomas Merton, who from 1939 to 1941 taught English at the college. Merton often crossed the railroad bridge over the river to climb the hills opposite campus, and according to local legend the heart-shaped opening was his favorite overlook. Yet it seems unlikely to have been especially attractive to him in actuality, having been created in the 1920s for the drilling of an oil well and installation of a pumpjack. Another local story has trees falling away in heart-shaped sorrow at the moment of his death in 1968. People on campus and in the surrounding community began evoking Merton in such legends or myths in the years after he left teaching, joined a monastery, and grew famous as a spiritual writer.

No story about Merton promises that a heart-shaped coppice will rise to sunshine, but wind has floated and deposited seeds, squirrels stashed nuts, brambles and shrubs and saplings poked skyward, and thin branches now dance in gusts of time in places where tall grass once bent in the Heart. The forest is edging into the opening, while to bears snuffling for sweet thimbleberries at the abandoned well site, humans on the distant campus must appear to scurry like delectable carpenter ants and cars to sheen like crunchy dung beetles. A few springs ago, I was canoeing the Allegheny opposite campus when I surprised bears on the muddy shoreline as they noshed wild carp seasoned with locally grown maggots, the sow huffing, muscling up the steep bank and waiting then at the grassy crest for the cubs before all three disappeared from my view, scrambling up to Merton's Heart—I like to imagine—to dig for chipmunks and enjoy the panorama.

In 2008, the property that encompasses the Heart was sold. The new owners have notified the university that hikers from campus are no longer welcome and that trespassers will be prosecuted. The bears seem pleased.

SKINNY DIPPING
WITH WILDLIFE

It sent me airborne with the shattering of the water and was gone from the surface before I realized it was a beaver. Within a week, it ceased tail whacking at the sight of me on the shore of my pond. It became very accustomed to me as it traveled to gather saplings for a lodge and cache of edible bark, and one evening it passed close as I fished from shore and as my dog stood up from a bed of grass. Another time it swam toward the dock on which I stood and twice looped around and beneath the planks. I spoke softly as it passed beneath me. It said nothing in reply. My words sounded ridiculous, even to me.

When the water had warmed enough in June for human swimming, my wife wondered whether it was a good idea for me to enter a pond to which a beaver had laid claim. A story had been in the news about a beaver that had climbed into a canoe and attacked a paddler. "That one in the paper must have had rabies," I said. "This is a friendly beaver."

Still, I didn't expect it to join my swim. But it did. I was over-whelmed, though I knew not by what exactly, just as I was back during March when the snow cover had yet to melt and a red-tailed hawk dipped within a hundred feet of me in pursuit of a squirrel, awesomely gliding and plush and varicolored in the rebounding sunlight, though, to the squirrel leaping from branch to branch in a spiraling rufous blur, the bird must have seemed something like the warplane Picasso implies in *Guernica*. Was it beauty that overwhelmed me? I hope not. A cavernous word, "beauty," one that can contain anything.

Since I was without trunks when the beaver joined my swim, I experienced an instant of cold contraction whenever it dove. Sometimes it surfaced ahead of me, sometimes behind, but never more than five or six yards away. My wife watched in astonishment from our kitchen window. I couldn't keep quiet. I told every relative, neighbor, and friend who I encountered later that day and week; I might even have accidentally used the word "beautiful." Some responded to my story by saying, "Oh, really?" or "No kidding?" I could tell that the "Oh, really?" and "No kidding?" ones assumed I was hyperbolizing. I have to admit that my story did sound ridiculous. Words sounded ridiculous.

The word "beaver" prompted one of my friends to make a lewd joke.

I felt a little sorry for him.

After that first time, the beaver joined me each time I went swimming. Whenever I treaded water, it floated nearby and sometimes drifted so near I could nearly touch it. Our sets of eyes almost level to each other inches above the water, I witnessed its blinking, its exhaling; it must have seen and heard me doing the same. I tried not to foolishly speak in its presence, but once in a while I succumbed.

It was August when the felling of saplings ceased and my dog lost interest in sniffing the packed mud and whittled branches where the lodge bridged water and land. Perhaps the beaver fell prey to a shoreline coyote, bobcat, or fisher, or abandoned my pond to seek a paddle-tailed companion, a better swimmer than I could hope to ever be. I swam alone until September when the leaves lost their gloss and the temperature of the pond made skinny dipping unthinkable.

A GOOD PLACE

My sap plummeting and years rattling, it swept me like an autumn storm. I was wearing shorts and a T-shirt and standing amidst a seesawing cloud of honeybees, and the acorns were still clinging, the apples only beginning to blush, and even though all of this was happening on an almost windless afternoon in August, I expected to see crinkled leaves and a few snowflakes blow past. People subject to panic attacks have told me their symptoms include jackhammering hearts and feverish gasping, but my panic was chilling. It was triggered by my awareness that the light was slanting into a syrupy late summer glow, which in turn caused me to notice that the irradiated heads of goldenrod were beginning to nod with nectar and the birdsong to mellow, reminders askance that my son would be starting kindergarten in September and that I had not always been going bald. After abbreviating my examination of my apiary and extinguishing the smudge fire in the bee smoker, I began to stride up my long gravel driveway, toward home, tilting into the imagined cold wind.

I felt we must visit the Adirondacks. I wondered how to explain my need to my wife as if our need: that our family must gather stores ahead of the winter gathering strength beyond the hills and pastures and woodlots of our home region—Adirondack tales of forested mountains, pristine lakes, the calls of loons, us—because whatever warm qualities home possessed in southwestern New York, it could not thaw my panic. In the Adirondacks and for a while after returning home with stores of stories, we might feel permanence. Our family would remain unchanged despite the altering of our home region: the new weekend homes sprouting on parceled land that was once farm meadow, the anxious blinking of another hilltop cell tower, the howling of chainsaws used to clear new parcels or harvest timber. The loggers and builders covet the Adirondacks as well, but are held at bay by the clause in the New York State Constitution that the Adirondack Park shall remain wilderness. The clause says "forever wild."

Forever.

The summer of my afternoon panic was the first I took my family to the Adirondacks. Hope was seven and Gabriel five years old. And until recent years we spent a week of every summer on wilderness waters, gathering memories that might last until our voices are forgotten by all who knew us. On the morning following that first of my summer chills, I threw a half-inflated inner tube atop our compact car and over that strapped down a dented aluminum canoe, a youth-camp discard that when younger and childless and much stronger I carried for five kilometers on a portage in Ontario's Algonquin Park. Surviving the big trucks on the New York State Thruway—rocking us as if we were already afloat—our family reached North Lake within six hours. My wife, Margaret, took the bow, our dog Gracie and I the stern, and the children squeezed side by side on one of the two vinyl canoe-packs. The seasons for black and deer flies had passed, it was sunny, and we saw no other watercraft between us and the distant green of shore. On water, I felt grounded.

We found a good site for camping between the lake and a granite basin worn smooth by a brook where our son could throw stones and launch stick boats of mossy spruce. It soon became evident that our daughter had a talent for imitating loons, and one night I woke to their cries and hers and crawled from the tent to find her at the nudged shoreline, the beam of her flashlight skating the lake as she conversed with birds in a language as mysterious to me as the Gaelic Irish she would much later learn to speak. Nose damp and lifted and twitching, our dog was in canine heaven all week, reading closely the molecules of creatures and place, eyes bright; ten years later would find her blind and miserable, and on an autumn afternoon I would lead her from our home and return alone, in my shaky grip a .22 caliber rifle. Margaret and I took dozens of photographs at the lake, but none did justice to our store of stories.

During the five-hour drive home, eight miles from home, on a sharp curve of a state highway, and despite the quart thermos bottle of coffee and the jabbering radio and the open driver-side window and my confidence in my consciousness, I fell asleep. Margaret seized the steering wheel and shouted me away from death.

Summers passed and Margaret lost her enthusiasm for rainy day paddling and greasy bug repellant and freeze-dried grub and smoky hair and realized that with the rest of us away she could vacation nicely at home. So the children and I went on canoeing and camping. And I confess that now when I speak the names of the waters we visited in the Algonquin and Adirondack parks, I feel the peace that I assume is felt by supplicants as they murmur the Our Father. *Little Clear Pond and Bear Pond and Kit Fox Pond and Lost Pond and Big Crow Lake.* The sounds transport me in two directions simultaneously, one with memories and one with plans, as if time has been abolished and I exist in an endless summer of map and compass. On one clear morning, our camping site on Lake Lila was visited by a leech-laden snapping turtle that kicked and wriggled its backside into sand between boulders beyond enormous white pines, and that evening, when loons beckoned my daughter to the shore, the prehistoric creature had departed, having deposited leathery eggs to be hatched under a blanket of sand warmed by an Adirondack summer.

A nd then a summer arrived when the children had left home for good and I was left to paddle alone. My plan was to put in on the West Branch of the Sacandaga River in the Adirondacks, weave to an alder-crowded tributary, cross Good Luck Lake, bushwhack to a hiking trail, continue my carry to Spectacle Lake, and there find a suitable campsite. That was the plan, but while still on the river I was caught in a gusty downpour. On the first suitable spot I found along Good Luck, I set about pitching my tent, the rainfly slapping my cold wet face until I could stake down the ties. The next morning, I woke to good weather. After drinking a cup of instant coffee, I circled the small lake in my canoe and learned I was the only human about, and decided to hang clothing out to dry and stay in the company of a loon couple on Good Luck.

When paddling alone in the Adirondacks or Algonquin, I sometimes am trailed and buzzed and bitten by the notion that a wilderness lake would be a good place to die, my body launched overboard by a coronary, feasted on by crawfish and bullheads, finally a sort of permanence. I swat away the thought.

A good place to die, my ass.

A good place to live.

After pride, cometh the hunger. I never pack enough foil packages of Tangy Fresh Marinara Spaghetti and Chef's Choice Beef Stew and Delectable Chicken Alfredo, counting on my fishing skills to keep me in enough calories when on a canoe trip. It is not that I dislike the risibly named, freeze-dried meals I reconstitute into hot mush; after a day of wilderness paddling, even boiled leather would taste good. Rather, it seems to me that a person camping on the shore of a lake and who witnesses ospreys and eagles rise with fish wriggling in talons ought to fill his gut with fresh protein if for no other reason than to dispel whatever romantic illusions such a person might harbor about the wildlife. Yet he is not always as good a self-provider as he might suppose himself to be.

Near the end of an extended stay on Little Tupper Lake in the Adirondacks, I found myself confined to land by strong wind, the expanse of whitecaps calling to my mind the swirling and drifting of snow—and was unable to catch a fish until the water calmed shortly before nightfall of my second consecutive day ashore. Since lunchtime I had eaten only a handful of raisins and a strip of venison jerky. At dusk I began casting a jitterbug, a stout and glug-glugging surface lure, making many foodless retrieves until, the lake black by then, I heard a splash and jerked upward the tip of my rod, setting the hooks of the jitterbug. I reeled the bass toward my net faster than I should have but, fortunately for me, without breaking the monofilament line. I prepared to fillet dinner on a flat, shoreline stone, but paused when I saw a glimmering within the beam of my head lamp, life emerging from the gaping mouth of the killed bass. A tail fin, faintly quivering. With my index finger and thumb, I pulled out a living sunfish and swung it outward and heard the splash, but it was a moonless night and my lamp too weak for me to learn whether Jonah could still swim.

SONGS

I.

Since someday a medical test could discover within you the thing long feared, the doctor's office might be a good setting for the beginning of this story. Yet this story has insisted on beginning weeks earlier when my wife and I were traveling to her maternal family reunion and I recalled flowers we had seen decades before that. We were in dairy country, the Herefords lying beneath thick clouds, and after passing several barns of almost black hemlock that made brilliant the white farmhouses against the gnawed timothy and heaps of dung and raggedly wooded hills, I pictured the enormous field of sunflowers we passed on a journey made decades earlier, all those golden-laced bonnets, heads bowed in prayer over a table that ended where it met blue sky. As I recalled the flowers, I suddenly supposed the cause of Margaret's mysterious illness.

"What's wrong?"

"Oh, nothing."

"Something's wrong. You look upset. What is it?"

"Nothing," I said. "Nothing's wrong."

Despite her ferocity in any fight, Margaret was losing her struggle against invasive fatigue and absconding memory. By the time her doctor told her that he could find no cause of her symptoms and suspected she had the baffling and untreatable condition known as chronic fatigue syndrome, her inner forearms were purple and puffed from the many laboratory extractions. I was worried he had missed something more dangerous and told him about Margaret's remove at her father's funeral months earlier, where she was like a small, dry island amidst a bog. She had been someone who would weep at the wake of a stranger—say, a sibling of some guy who taught second grade up the hall from her—but during the doleful warm-up music at her father's send-off, she leaned against me on the pew and whispered, "He had one foot in the grave and the other on a banana peel. Then he slipped."

After my funeral anecdote the doctor said, "Maybe they had a relationship problem."

I asked about a brain scan.

"Probably unnecessary," he said. "Maybe later," he said.

He ordered a psychological evaluation.

Now she and I were nearing her family reunion in her cousin's backyard in a small town in western New York.

We were late because that morning she had taken nearly an hour to dress: I had already put the cooler in the car when I found her sitting on the edge of our bed with one leg in her jeans and then, fifteen minutes later, still only one leg. When I steered the car onto her cousin's driveway, Margaret's eyes were closed. I squeezed her shoulder. She asked, "Are we there yet?"

Out on the gravel, I smelled sizzling blood and fat. I said, "Hurry up."

On our way to the family reunion, I had been remembering how we got to the flowers. We saw them during the long journey we planned shortly after I told her I had been offered a university teaching assistantship out in North Dakota. She had responded, "So are we getting married?"

"Are you pregnant?"

Despite my obnoxious question, our children would be undreamt for a decade. To reach North Dakota, we traveled a day and much of a night through New York and Pennsylvania and Ohio and Michigan and Wisconsin, belongings squeezed into a rusty sedan, a bank check representing our pooled savings of under a grand stuffed in the glove compartment with the registration and map and the wedding cards from kin who back then were yet alive. We felt rich, or as we assumed the rich felt. We talked almost nonstop even after nightfall, and in the background the DJ blather and rock music and jingling sales pitches and the bad news that could never catch us came and went on the radio like the flashing of lightning bugs back East.

She parked the car on a wide shoulder of U.S. Route 2 when we were exhausted. We moved a large box of winter clothing from between us into the passenger seat so we could sleep propped upright against each other, swaying to the gusts of big trucks. We woke to dawn in western Minnesota and saw that we edged a field of sunflowers which faded into horizon. I peed on gravel. She took her turn. We soon were back on the road, and soon she must have said, "You're speeding."

Hungrily lifting its multitude of heads, the great field intoned *amen.*

Several weeks after the reunion, an optometrist found that Margaret's field of vision was splattered with blind spots, and he explained without surprising me that the cause was not in her eyes. It was "somewhere behind the eyes."

He sent a report to her doctor, to sink in somewhere behind his eyes.

On the wall opposite my wife and her sister and me, and behind the doctor, a pharmaceutical advertisement brightly illustrated a diseased bodily organ. He was talking about the CAT scan he had ordered. He was young and pudgy. He stood in place but rocked slightly like a beach ball on the verge of rolling away in a breeze. I had expected to hear the diagnosis in singular, but he kept using the plural. *Tumors, tumors.* Margaret's sister and I asked questions that sped his rocking. Margaret didn't speak from her seat.

I rose early and somewhat unrested on the morning after the day of the hard seats. I peed on the lawn and stretched in milky light. I dressed. I ate eggs and toast and then finished a cup of strong coffee as I checked email. I again went outside and trailed my dog around our pond while from high pasture a John Deere barked at us. The sun floated orange near the horizon. A hillside grove of pine shed faint mist.

Margaret was still in bed as noon neared, curled on her side, leg draped over a ball of blanket. Standing at the foot of the bed, I launched into what I liked to insist was our song. When I serenaded her with Rod Stewart's "Maggie May"—"*Wake up, Maggie, I think I got something to say to you*"—my artistry normally received from her some veiled criticism. Such as, "*Oh—please shut up!*"

I stopped myself as I realized verses neared that, this time, I should suppress. Yet, this time, her eyes still closed, she whispered them: "All you did was wreck my bed. And in the morning kick me in the head."

II.

Two weeks before the surgery, she visited with our daughter in Manhattan. One night while she was away, I brought home a green bottle of Jameson whiskey. The dog eventually rose from the carpet, beckoned me to the front door by scratching at it urgently, hastened out, lay on the cold September lawn, and would come back inside only after my howling ceased.

III.

During the worry-filled predawn ride to the cancer institute up in Buffalo—our car funneled by a glacial valley past the faded billboards and dim diners and homemade "Deer Processing" signs along sinuous NY Route 16, the hills still dark, October foliage unseen—I recalled a story about my grandfather Barley Phillips and the first of his eight children, Sam. It had been told to me by my short-lived father and two of my long-lived uncles, each of whom added to it bars of his own tune. It always begins with throbbing, which has become so strong that Sam can no longer work as a draftsman. And he tells Barley why. Barley says there is some mistake. Sam adds that a second doctor made the same diagnosis. "Well—you can get better. Right?"

He stares at his father across the table for a long moment. "I dunno, Pop. Who do you know who ever got better from brain cancer?" He shrugs. He looks away. "I guess I can hope. I mean— my kid."

"You'll get better." Barley stands and moves very slowly to a cupboard. He removes two mugs. Sam shrugs again. He stands.

He shrugs once more. He follows his father down the cellar steps to the tapped barrel.

The next day, when Barley calls in sick, the foreman kids him. "Nice morning. Going fishing?"

A suggestion is made that the foreman should fish the phone out of his colon.

Late in the morning, father and son listen as the man with the long and unblemished fingers explains the surgery. Finally he asks, "Do you have any questions?"

"No. I guess not. No."

"Me neither. But I just want you to know I've decided I'm gonna watch you operate."

"I beg your pardon?"

"You'll be more sure to be careful with my son."

During the surgery, Barley watches from above, through glass in the floor, a security guard at his side. He sees the shaven scalp peeled, the skull reminding him of the mysterious domed mosques he has seen in pictures. He sees the searchers, who are locked out of the mosque, cut through the wall and lift away a section. He sees them enter the interior that throbs with watery music, curtsy and circle, and lead out with utmost courtesy, what little of it they can, the interloper.

I thought again about my grandfather and his eldest child while Margaret was under the knife, strangely solaced by the cadences of the ancestral fugue, even sleeping for a while on the waiting room seat, although I woke thinking no longer about Barley and Sam. I woke feeling like the hare caught by the tortoise. "Are we there yet?" the tortoise asked.

Wondering, I rubbed my eyes.

IV.

About two weeks after the surgery, a doctor reported that one tumor was benign and the other an unrelated malignancy that might or might not have spread. He added a caveat. The cancerous "might" was more mighty than the "might not." The pathology report reminded Margaret and me of those corny good-news, bad-news jokes, and eventually we joked without laughing about the unintentional truth from Bill Clinton that much "depends upon what the meaning of the word is is."

The benign growth—how benign is the meaning of *benign*?— had hugged the optic nerve and the pituitary or "master" gland, and the malignancy had squatted in her frontal lobe. Eventually Margaret was under the care of an oncologist, radiation oncologist, endocrinologist, hematologist, ophthalmologist, and neurologist; and one of them informed us "the chance is good" the cancer would reappear within ten years. *Good?* Another specialist was tall and good-humored and stood in the middle of the examination room, while the assisting nurse stood near the wall opposite Margaret's and my seats, and informed Margaret that the most recent MRI looked normal except where the tumors had been; he said, "Now you're holey." I asked how long it might be before the cancer returned. He didn't say ten years. He said three. He paused for a few seconds, looking at the floor, and then said, "But it doesn't have to come back." Was the cancer on a leave of absence? Yet another specialist said with an encouraging lilt that among her patients with the type of tumor cut from Margaret's frontal lobe, "One has been cancer-free for three years."

I succumbed to fear of the unknown. In a panicked seeking of survival statistics from treatment studies, I telephoned the cancer institute where the surgery had been performed, hoping that numbers could heal the cleaved meanings of words. I spoke with a nurse practitioner familiar with Margaret's case; like the various doctors caring for my wife, the practitioner was empathetic but finally said, because I insisted, that speculating about Margaret's future "would be like not knowing if the weather and traffic are good or bad and then trying to predict how many red lights you will hit later that day on Niagara Falls Boulevard."

I was sitting at the kitchen table, bent as if saying grace, jamming the receiver against my ear as if trying to penetrate my skull, attending her tones and rhythms and words as if she were the Pythia.

> *Lights*
> *will*
> *hit.*

V.

So far—for over five years now—the MRI report issued each four months has characterized Margaret's brain as *stable*, a nice enough word and with a clear meaning when applied to inanimate objects. Yet tell us, Doctor, if you would, what my wife's *is* is.

When some kind friend or acquaintance asks me how Margaret "is" or "is doing," I usually say, "She's okay." I actually mean that while waiting for the results of another MRI, she feels like a character in Shirley Jackson's "The Lottery"; and that five times a day she swallows pills which slightly boost memory and concentration, imperfectly replace several hormones, and diminish the threats of seizures and thrombosis; and that her postsurgical history of clotting prevents her from taking the estrogen needed to slow the worsening of her spinal osteoporosis; and that because of her damaged ability to concentrate, she can't drive even though enough of her vision has returned.

When we made stew one afternoon this past winter, she took about twenty minutes to prepare four carrots for the pot. Each motion took her several times longer than it would have before the cancer: each slow sweep of the peeler, shifting of a carrot, pressing of the knife, gathering of slices, each of those slow movements followed by a pause. That evening, I called her to the kitchen table where I had lined up pills, but a grocery receipt distracted her and she read through it again and again. She then became distracted by the instructions on the back of an electric knife sharpener we had owned for years, reading them repeatedly. "Take the pills," I kept urging. If I hadn't, an hour later the pills would have waited.

Margaret is and is not who Margaret is.

I have gone from none to two beers per day before the cancer to none to four after. As for Margaret, whose medications make any amount of alcohol hazardous, she seems not to miss the occasional drink—even though, all those years ago when we were on our first date, she challenged me to a beer-chugging contest. After winning second place, I learned she had read those long, long Russian novels that intimidated me. They still do. She can no longer work as a teacher but somehow finishes more books than ever, though she reads with lips moving as if in prayer, can tell me little about plots and characters, and might begin the same novel a month later as if knowing it only from a review. I would like to read *My Ántonia* once each month if I could keep forgetting the fate of the Shimerdas and Jim Burden and Lena Lingard, but not if I would misplace the word *book*. "Did you see where I left it?" she asks at least once a day.

"Left what?"

"You know—it, *it*."

But her long-term memory is better than mine, her oneiric new days draining around solid old times, like steaming water around potatoes in a strainer. Over dinner, she recently asked whether I remembered her meeting my mother. I didn't. She reported that it was on a snowy evening in March and my mother was boiling potatoes and the kitchen windows were steamed.

Unlike the thin frosty stubble of my pate, her regrown hair is still dark, and occasionally, momentarily, in dim light, she looks to me as she did when decades ago I first glimpsed her: at an ice skating rink, before I knew even her name. That long moment ago. Late one recent evening, she shut off the lamp at the couch and I gazed up from my reading in the easy chair across the room and she saw in my look what I saw. She waited until I began to read again before asking whether I recalled when we spent a rainy spring weekend at a cabin and built a fire and "stayed in bed all day."

"I remember just the all-day part," I replied—proudly.

"You were such a pig."

Despite her drastically changed life, she says she will be happy as long as she is without cancer, but I'm unsure whether *happy* and *sad* still mean to her anything similar to what they mean to me. Some of her emotional range was restored by the surgery, but tragedy seems unable to move her. Back when we were still childless and watched the film *Sophie's Choice*, she wept when a Nazi forced Sophie to choose whether her daughter or son would survive the Shoah, but while recently re-watching the scene in our home where we had raised a good daughter and son, Margaret looked as if she were listening to a Dow Jones Industrial report. When she told me that one of her beloved cousins had cancer, her tone was suggestive of a weather report. *Four to eight inches of snow overnight.* When she finished reading a draft of this essay, she said, "It's fine," and asked, "Are you making anything for supper?"

A while back, she began repeating some of her statements in singsong. Especially, "I don't know, *I don't know-ho!*" She soon commenced the uttering of morphemic gibberish, streams of which sound like prayers in a strange language when voiced quietly, and dissonant songs when loudly. On some days these vocalizations are frequent when she is unoccupied by conversation or reading or film. She might punctuate them with bursts of words in English—"*Oh yeah! Oh yeah!*"—and the brief clapping of hands and swaying of torso and stomping of feet. She is at times unaware of her sounds and dance but at others is "singing a real song in my head."

What does *real* really mean? Her doctors aren't sure, but they say the definition might be found in her sliced and radiated frontal lobe.

VI.

Years before the hours of surgery and weeks of radiation and months of chemotherapy and even the first symptoms of trouble, a fall from the sky startled me as I stood in our yard watching a mallard on the pond. I thought the eagle had missed, although probably its intention was to flush the duck off the water. The second one ripped the prey from midair sunshine. The eagle pair then undulated off while one sheening blue feather seesawed downward, raptor heads and tails rapturous, brightly white as patches of snow in sunshine, circling behind tall pines and out of my view. For a little longer, I heard the drake's rhythmic squawking.

VII.

I made a confession to my wife this past December. It was after she asked me to cut a fir and buy a potted poinsettia. The children would be home soon and she wanted the house to look as they remembered it to be on Christmas. She was in a rocking chair near the wood stove and I in another in a corner of the living room, books in laps—Ma and Pa Kettle, a little prematurely—and between us the dog was asleep on the carpet, which badly needed cleaning. I don't fully understand why after so many years I chose that evening to confess and why of all my faults and wrongs, of all the apologies I maybe should make, I chose that one.

"I have a confession."

"Oh, brother. What?"

I was remembering she and I had dated several months when my uncle Al suggested I "take her out to a good restaurant"—and handed me thirty bucks, a lavish amount to a kid who thought of classy restaurants as those eateries which did not serve hot dogs—and that two evenings later, a department store tie clipped to my collar, I bowed and handed her a bouquet as I picked her up from her home, disguised as a gentleman. Now—in our home of thirty years—I asked whether she remembered that first time I gave her flowers.

"Of course," she said. "So what's your big confession?"

I confessed I had gathered them from the cemetery near my mother's house, a few from each of several graves so no one else would notice. Maybe so none of me would be in her largest blind spot, she studied me askance. The fire was nearly out, but it was a warm night, considering the month. "You're something."

I nodded.

Again she paused askance, reminding me of a robin stalking breakfast, one eye fixed on earthworm, the other on sky, whispering in her new language as if she had forgotten about me—"*ah sah lah ooo ish ish*"—and then was silent a while before using the language we still shared. Out of the right corner of my right eye, I saw a faint, creamy orange glow emanating from behind the thick glass of the stove door. "Well," she said, "I think they were still kind of pretty anyhow."

ABSOLUTION

If a novelist were to have his protagonist reading *The Plague* mere hours before learning that his wife has brain cancer, the irony would be cheap, a postmodernist Henny Youngman joke. Yet I was indeed reading Camus's novel on the day when I would learn that Margaret, my wife, had cancer—though not entirely by coincidence. I'd first read it at eighteen when my father was close to death from cancer, and then again when I was thirty and my donation of a kidney failed to save my sister's life. It sounds morbid to sum up events this way, but it hadn't felt like that. After the deadly contagion in Oran fades, and the quarantine is lifted, the doctor-narrator of *The Plague* marvels at how quickly survivors resume their old outlook; in my case, my sister had been dead only a few weeks when I slipped back into the comfortable shoes of my old life, and Death once again became a character in stories about other families. I didn't reopen *The Plague* until after Margaret became ill.

I'm no longer angry at the doctor who misdiagnosed her cancer as chronic fatigue syndrome. Probably an earlier scan would have made little difference, and regardless, I shouldn't blame anyone for her bad luck and I have no interest in picking a fight with God. Whenever I am inclined to scapegoat, I recall the priest in

The Plague who blamed victims for their fate, pronouncing the contagion a divine punishment for the sins of Adam and Eve. And whenever I seek escape, such as drinking too much alcohol, I force myself to remember the journalist in *The Plague* who tried to cajole and bribe his way out of the quarantine.

Yet I never finished my third reading of *The Plague*. I left it shut after that morning when my wife and I sat in the doctor's office and heard the word *tumors*, feeling like Adam and Eve learning that never again would they eat from the tree of life. Mortality is more emotionally troublesome and less intellectually newsworthy to me now than when I was eighteen or thirty years old; and I don't mean mine, but rather the mortality of my loved ones. Without them, the temporal limits of my life would matter little. While Margaret dozed on the couch one evening, her head resting on my shoulder, it struck me, as I thought about my closed copy of *The Plague,* that just as Hannah Arendt has made it banal to say that evil is banal, the existentialists have made it absurd to dwell on absurdity. The third chapter in Genesis fails to convince me that we must die because of sin, but at least it attempts an answer. What is the enemy against which Camus urges our struggle?

The Plague is as perfect as that butterfly in the graveyard near the end of James Agee's autobiographical novel *A Death in the Family.* Yet I have lacked the courage to finish my third reading. Margaret is braver than her husband, which should be unsurprising to anyone even abstractly aware that women have endured everything men have ever endured, while also enduring men. In the days following her diagnosis, the only fear she expressed was concerning the damage to her optic nerve by one of the tumors. "If I live," she said to me one night in the darkness in bed, "I hope I have my eyesight when my grandchildren are born. Those beautiful, beautiful babies."

On a Sunday, months after the surgery, an acquaintance from a different town called to ask whether he was welcome to stop by with members of his church so they could place their hands on my wife and pray for her. Margaret replied that God knew enough of her without people describing to Him her contours, but our well-meaning acquaintance persisted, warning that the devil causes human suffering and that healing can occur only when the Lord has been properly beseeched. "No thanks," she said. "But if God Himself ever wants to put His hands on me, maybe I'll be in the mood."

When they involve no touching of her by strangers, Margaret welcomes prayers. Yet usually such offerings cause me to think about unanswered prayers; for example, the millions of urgent prayers of intercession for the people trapped on the upper floors of the burning Twin Towers. A former coworker contacted me to say she had heard about my wife's misfortune and was praying for her, but acknowledged happily the earthly limits of prayer; should the disease prove fatal, the Lord will have shown "He loves Margaret so much He wants her near Him in Heaven."

My wife says that by praying for her health, people are sharing love. I once wondered aloud whether people pray for her in part because any of them could fall mortally ill at any moment and they need to comfort themselves with the belief that prayers can cure what doctors cannot. She asked, "And who loves purely? Are you telling me you do?"

In his famous commencement address given at Kenyon College, David Foster Wallace reminded his listeners that everyone worships something. I am reminded of his speech when I am in a pharmacy and observe customers fingering bottles of vitamins and herbs as if they are rosary beads. I think of it as I cross the parking lot of my local YMCA and look up to see the sweating, huffing people beyond the glass front of the second floor as they pedal stationary bikes devotedly, fervently. When someone advises Margaret to give up sugar or avoid cell phone radiation or to drink green tea or eat more broccoli, I am reminded of the acquaintance whose church members hope to drive satanic cancer from my wife and instill salvation. A different acquaintance warned us that stress causes cancer; and to protect me from stress-induced plague, Margaret said to me, "She means well."

I too supposed the cause, though not the salvation. Margaret grew up near a large commercial orchard and both of her parents smoked tobacco. I thought I knew the answer when I asked one of her doctors whether childhood exposure to pesticides or secondhand smoke might have caused the malignancy. He replied, "We have no evidence that any of those chemicals cause her type of cancer. The cause is unknown."

My wife eventually permitted someone other than doctors and family to lay hands on her. Her sister had given her a wig and Margaret wanted it altered. The hairdresser explained that she needed to know whether it was made with natural or synthetic hair and would need to check the underside to be certain. Would Margaret like to go into the women's room with her to remove the wig in more privacy? "Just take it off here," said Margaret. When the hairdresser turned the wig inside out and examined it in the bright lighting, everyone in the salon could see the long purplish scar that began near one of Margaret's ears and then slalomed over her head just inside the hairless hairline. When the wig was back in place, the hairdresser began her expert trimming and styling. My wife and I live in the Alleghenies, in hardscrabble logging and dairy country where any hairdresser finds it difficult to earn even a bare living from standing on her feet all day and applying her special skill, and yet, on this day, this hairdresser declined to accept payment.

Margaret insisted. From the waiting area, I insisted. The hairdresser took Margaret's head gently in her hands. "No," she said, "there's no charge."

EPILOGUE

The maples crimson, oaks yet green, ash already naked. Margaret and I and our Brittany Spaniel Jenny are crossing high pasture along yet higher woodland. The pasture drops precipitously to level ground where it is crevassed by a stony stream and separated from the barnyard and lawns of the Swift place by a post and wire fence line. Below us, cattle whip themselves with their tails, laggardly since fly season is past, and occasionally lift their heads to check our progress. Over the decades, we have walked this place with our children, now grown and living far from home, and one after the other with our earlier dogs Franny and Nectar and Gracie. And now with Jenny.

We used to dream in straight forward lines on our hikes.

Now in loops.

My neighbor Bob Swift is probably watching television in his parlor down there, as he usually is these days when I visit him in the homestead. Nine decades ago, in the same house, he was born on the kitchen table. His health is no longer good enough for him to be a full-time dairy farmer—the cattle are owned by his daughter Dawn—and that's what bothers him the most about his age, that he can no longer work from morning to night, baling hay, or cleaning cow stalls, or plowing fields, or chopping corn, or tending fence line, though, on some cool clear days, when his breathing is less wheezy and joints not so pained, he still helps Dawn and her husband with barn chores.

Many stories of work and survival will be lost when Bob dies. When he was a boy, he would hike up the big steep pasture and then uphill more through forest and then curve downward along cropland owned by a different family to reach the one-room schoolhouse where reading, writing, civics, and arithmetic were taught. Each year in early spring when the garlicky wild leeks had poked up from the woodland humus, he ate of their oval greens and smooth white bulbs on his way to school so that his breath would foul the room and the teacher would send him home, where he joined happily his father in the fields or barn. He remembers when he and his father would use a crosscut saw to cut their firewood. He remembers when electricity first came to these hills, shortly after the vast bloodshed of World War Two. He has sowed and reaped for nine decades on a land where the Seneca of the Iroquois Confederation once hunted with bow and arrow and from which one of his ancestors left to enter the bloodshed of the Civil War.

Eventually Bob would witness the scattering of land over the caskets of his grandparents and parents and siblings—and, even so, in his many years before that especially hard day in spring 2017 when land was scattered over the casket of his wife, Elaine, he would hold his four children and dozens of grandchildren and great-grandchildren, new life in the arms of someone long ago a newborn.

I recall some of Bob's stories each time I cross his pasture.

His stories loop mine.

If Margaret dies before I do, I will lose my bearings on this land of stories. She has difficulty remembering what happened only hours earlier, and tends to confuse what occurred today with what did several days ago, but her long-term memory is better than mine. It is late in the evening as we hike the pasture and she asks whether I know when the next full moon will be. I don't. She then asks whether I recall the night when Hope, our daughter, was a toddler and noticed a full moon and pointed at it from the picture window in our kitchen.

I shake my head.

"You don't?"

I do. But I reply, "No." I desire to know the story again, from her, as we move forward together.

"It was fall." Margaret glances back and forth between the land ahead and me. "She didn't know how to say it. We bundled her up and took her outside. We already had snow." Although she is slightly out of breath from our hike, her voice rises with annoyance at my apparent failure of memory. "She was so excited and kept pointing up and calling the moon *bakah*. You must remember? Don't you?"

"Yes," I say. "I remember now. Bakah."

Surely we have hiked the pasture at least fifty times over the years—just for the view. The first was while we were dating, and Richard Nixon had resigned the presidency to avoid impeachment for high crimes; we hiked it after Bill Clinton was impeached for lying under oath about having sex with a twenty-two-year-old intern in the Oval Office; and we hike it now when our president is a proud bigot, mocks the handicapped, boasts about his sexual assaults on women, and has a man-crush on the dictator of Russia. The economy and the land have changed, but not the prevalence of scoundrels in our government, and it could be that the American people have not changed either. Perhaps as an old saying has it, we get the government we deserve.

Yet here on upper pasture under a generally clear sky and in the mingled odors of timothy and fallen leaves and cow dung and the dusky shrilling and rasping of crows, jays, and blackbirds, no politics.

We can see several houses along the low winding black thread of road and also see two people out in a yard, perhaps raking leaves, gender and skin color unrecognizable so far away, humans tiny and ethereal on the ancient land. I suppose they are sweating as they rake. The air temperature feels to be in the sixties despite the season. Although we see none, crickets are calling to each other; it sounds like thousands of them, so many that for a while I stop noticing the birdcalls and the grassy crunching of my footsteps; the crickets sound like heavy rain first striking dry fallen leaves. Now that the sun is behind the lowland forest that forms some of the western border of the pasture, out of the west, over the treetops, streaks of crimson flow and coagulate. We turn, hastening toward home, our breathing harder, enjoying the urgency as below us the cattle make their way to the barn.

Jenny lopes and loops ahead of us, her ears and tongue flapping like small flags, glancing back periodically to see if Margaret and I are keeping up. Although her joy appears tireless, Jenny has a leaky heart valve as a consequence of her heart physically enlarging as it works harder in her old age. The same can happen to a human heart, and—who knows, who with certainty can say otherwise—it might be that all human hearts can enlarge better and more than physically. At least how can *I* say otherwise? As Margaret, I, and our dog rush ahead of darkness, here where our shared years have seemed a miracle, more, more, we long for more.